PAKISTAN TRAVEL GU

Pakistan Travel Guide 2023

Experience the Splendor of Pakistan; Where Adventure, History, and Culture Converge

Travis D. Marrero

PAKISTAN TRAVEL GUIDE 2023

Copyright © 2023 Travis D. Marrero

All rights reserved. No part of this publication may be reproduced, distributed, or transmitted in any form or by any means, including photocopying, recording, or other electronic or mechanical methods, without the prior written permission of the publisher, except in the case of brief quotations embodied in critical reviews and certain other noncommercial uses permitted by copyright law.

PAKISTAN TRAVEL GUIDE 2023

Table Of Contents

Welcome To Pakistan
Introduction to Pakistan
Geography and Climate
Culture and History
Politics and Government
Economy

Chapter 1: Preparing For Your Trip
Travel Documents and Visa Requirements
Safety and Health Advice
Important Items To Pack
Exchange Rates and Money
Access To The Internet And Communication

Chapter 2: How To Reach Pakistan
Airlines and Airports
Border Crossings on Land
Ferries and Sea Ports

Chapter 3: Exploring the Pakistani Regions
Capital Territory of Islamabad
Punjab Province

PAKISTAN TRAVEL GUIDE 2023

Sindh Province
Province of Khyber Pakhtunkhwa
Balochistan Province
Region of Gilgit-Baltistan
Region of Azad Jammu and Kashmir

Chapter 4: Major Cities and Vacation Spots

Chapter 5: Cultural and Historical Places
UNESCO World Heritage Sites
Archeological Ruins
Archeological Ruins
Palaces and Forts
Shrines and Mosques
Museums and Art Galleries
Events and Festivals of Culture

Chapter 6: Natural Wonders and Outdoor Adventures
Trekking & Hiking
Climbing and Mountaineering
Wildlife Refuges And National Parks
Lakes and Rivers
Coastal Regions and Beaches

PAKISTAN TRAVEL GUIDE 2023

Dunes and Deserts
Caves and Waterfalls

Chapter 7: Traditional Foods and Regional Specialties
Well-known Pakistani Recipes
Snacks and Street Food
Customary Drinks and Foods
Food Manners and Dining Rituals

Chapter 8: Purchases and Souvenirs
Traditional Crafts and Visual Arts
Bazaars and Markets
Shopping Centers and Malls
Special Merchandise to Take Home

Chapter 9: Transportation Within Pakistan
Internal Air Travel
Railroads and Trains
Coaches and Buses
Ride-Sharing and Taxi Services

Chapter 10: Pakistan's Accommodation Options

Resorts and Inns
Hostels and Guesthouses
Homestays and Farm Stays
Camping and Glamping

Chapter 11: Advise and Cultural Etiquette
Salutations and Social Manners
Modesty and Dress Code
Communication and Language
Religious Customs and Protocol
Safety Precautions and Ethical Tourism

Chapter 12: Events and Festivals
Muslim Holidays
Public Holidays and Other National Events
Local and Regional Celebrations
Sports Competitions and Events

Chapter 13: Useful Phrases and Basic Urdu Vocabulary

Chapter 14: Emergency Information
Emergency Numbers and Contacts
Medical Facilities and Services

PAKISTAN TRAVEL GUIDE 2023

Consulates and Embassies

Conclusion

PAKISTAN TRAVEL GUIDE 2023

Welcome To Pakistan

Welcome to the Pakistan Travel Guide 2023! I am pleased to share my travel experiences with you since I have firsthand knowledge of the allure and beauty of Pakistan. You'll discover advice and insights from my remarkable trip across this fascinating nation inside the pages of this book.

My stay in Pakistan was a life-changing trip, rich in kind people, beautiful scenery, and cultural riches. Every moment in Pakistan offered the promise of exploration and amazement, from the mighty mountains that appeared to reach the skies to the busy towns humming with life.

I traveled around the various areas, taking in the vibrant cities of Lahore and Karachi, the calm beauty of Islamabad, and the fascinating history of Peshawar. While the colorful bazaars flooded my senses with the fragrances of spices and the vivid colors of handicrafts, the ancient ruins and architectural wonders transported me back in time.

The stunning natural marvels of Pakistan are indescribable. The tranquil lakes tucked away among jagged rocks, the verdant valleys that seemed like they belonged in a fairy tale, and the immaculate beaches lapped by the Arabian Sea left me in amazement. The outdoor experiences, which ranged from thrilling excursions to meetings with unusual creatures, made a lasting impression on my psyche.

But it was the people of Pakistan who made my trip one to remember. My heart was struck by the sincere friendliness, compassion, and warmth I experienced wherever I visited. The relationships I made in Pakistan were priceless, from the kind locals who let me into their homes to the other travelers who became lifetime friends.

You'll discover not just useful advice on travel arrangements, lodging, and sights in this book, but also individual suggestions that perfectly reflect Pakistan. I cordially welcome you to go in my footsteps, to brave the uncharted, and to make your own priceless experiences in this amazing nation.

I urge you to approach each moment as you go off on your trip with an open heart and an open mind. Engage with the populace, savor the delights of genuine Pakistani food, and get fully immersed in the lively cultural fabric of this country. Leave only appreciation-inspired imprints on the environment and respect local traditions and customs.

May this travel guide be your dependable travel companion, pique your interest, and provide you with the knowledge you need to set off on an unforgettable vacation. Pakistan welcomes you with open arms and is eager to offer its history and hidden treasures. Prepare to write your page in Pakistan's intriguing story.

Wishing you treasured memories and wonderful adventures,

Travis D. Marrero

Introduction to Pakistan

Pakistan, sometimes referred to as the Islamic Republic of Pakistan, is a South Asian nation. India to the east, Afghanistan and Iran to the west, China to the north, and the Arabian Sea to the south make up its shared boundaries. It is the fifth-most populated nation in the world with a population of more than 220 million. Pakistan's biggest city is Karachi, whereas Islamabad is the country's capital. Pakistan is a nation with a lively culture, a long history, a diversified terrain, a complicated political system, and an expanding economy. This chapter will examine a variety of Pakistani facets to provide readers with a thorough understanding of the nation.

Geography and Climate

Mountains, plateaus, plains, and deserts are all present in Pakistan's diversified topography. The Karakoram, Hindu Kush, and Himalayan mountain ranges, including K2, the second-highest peak in the world, dominate the northern region of the nation. From all over the world, these breathtaking mountains draw mountaineers and adventure seekers. In the north of Pakistan, there are breathtaking glaciers, clean lakes, and verdant valleys that add to its natural splendor.

The eastern and southern parts of the nation are covered by the rich Indus River plain, which is ideal for agriculture. The region's namesake, the huge Indus River, provided a lifeline for the civilization that flourished here thousands of years ago. The country's agricultural production is sustained by irrigation systems that are supported by the river. The lowlands are speckled with thriving towns, ancient ruins, and modern monuments.

The Balochistan Plateau, which is located to the west, is distinguished by its rocky and dry topography. In the southeast of the nation, this area merges with the huge Thar Desert, which is shared with India. The Thar Desert offers a look into the hard yet interesting desert lifestyle since it is a unique ecosystem with its distinctive flora and wildlife.

Pakistan's terrain and geographic characteristics result in a variety of climates. Winter (October to February), spring (March and April), summer (May to September), and fall (September and October) are the four main seasons. In coastal regions, the climate is dry, but in the northern highlands, it is moderate. While the northern parts have colder winters and cooler summers, the coastal districts along the Arabian Sea receive a mild maritime climate. From July through September, Pakistan also experiences monsoon rains, which are essential for recharging water supplies and supporting agriculture.

Culture and History

The history of Pakistan is lengthy and old, going back thousands of years. There is evidence of human occupancy in the area going back to the Paleolithic epoch, making it the birthplace of civilization. The Indus Valley Civilization, which peaked about 2500 BCE, was one of the most famous prehistoric civilizations to have existed in this area. The Indus Valley Civilization is recognized for its distinctive artifacts, well-developed drainage systems, and superior urban design.

The region that makes up modern-day Pakistan has been ruled by several emperors and dynasties throughout the years. During the third century BCE, the Maurya Empire, led by the renowned Mauryan Emperor Ashoka, exercised its power across the area. The Gupta Empire, which is renowned for its artistic and intellectual accomplishments, had a profound influence on the area.

When Islam was introduced to the Indian subcontinent in the eighth century CE, Muslim empires such as the Delhi Sultanate and the Mughal Empire began to flourish there. The Mughal Empire, which peaked during Emperor Akbar, had a lasting impression on the region's art, architecture, and cultural history. The Lahore Fort, Badshahi Mosque, and Shalimar Gardens are examples of Mughal architecture that bear witness to imperial splendor.

British colonial dominance over the Indian subcontinent began in the 18th and 19th centuries. In the 20th century, the fight against British imperialism gathered strength, which resulted in the partition of

India in 1947. Muhammad Ali Jinnah served as both the country's founder and its first Governor-General when Pakistan was established as a distinct, Muslim-majority country after being split off from British India.

Pakistan has a rich cultural past that has been influenced by its native customs, Islamic traditions, and the Mughal Empire's legacy. Numerous ethnic groups, each with its unique language, customs, and cuisine, call the nation home, including the Punjabis, Sindhis, Balochis, Pashtuns, and Mohajirs. Famous poets and authors have contributed to Pakistani culture's literary history, and the arts, literature, music, and dance are all thriving components of that culture. The creative prowess of the populace is shown in traditional crafts including ceramics, handwoven fabrics, and delicate needlework.

Pakistanis are renowned for their generous hospitality and a strong feeling of belonging. Festivals like Eid-ul-Fitr, Eid-ul-Adha, and Basant are joyfully observed and celebrated, bringing people together. The national sport of India, cricket, is very popular and acts as a uniting factor for the country.

Politics and Government

Pakistan has a democratic form of government and is a federal parliamentary republic. The head of government of Pakistan is the Prime Minister, whereas the head of state is the President. The National Assembly is the lower chamber of the Parliament, while the Senate is the upper house. An electoral college is made up of representatives from the provincial assembly and both chambers of Parliament elect the president.

Pakistan's political system is multi-party, with political parties standing for a variety of ideas and interests. Among the most well-known political parties in the nation are Pakistan Tehreek-e-Insaf (PTI), Pakistan Muslim League-Nawaz (PML-N), and Pakistan People's Party (PPP). Members of the National Assembly and provincial legislatures are chosen in general elections that take place every five years.

Throughout its history, Pakistan has seen periods of political unrest and military control. With several military coups and interventions, the military has significantly influenced the political landscape of the nation. However, Pakistan has made progress in recent years in enhancing its democratic institutions and making sure that the political process is more inclusive.

Economy

A developing economy, Pakistan's GDP is mostly derived from the sectors of agriculture, industry, and services. A considerable majority of the workforce is employed in the agriculture industry, which is also an important source of income for rural towns. The nation is renowned for the crops it produces, including wheat, rice, cotton, and sugarcane. Pakistan is one of the top manufacturers of textiles and apparel in the world, and its textile sector considerably boosts exports.

The industrial sector includes a variety of sectors, such as textile, chemical, cement, steel, pharmaceutical, and automobile manufacturing. Through programs like the China-Pakistan Economic Corridor (CPEC), which seeks to improve connectivity and infrastructure development between Pakistan and China, Pakistan has made attempts to entice international investment and encourage commerce.

With industries like information technology, telecommunications, banking, finance, and tourism playing a critical role in the economy, the services sector has seen tremendous expansion in recent years. Pakistan has a youthful, energetic labor population, and the country's IT industry has shown great promise, drawing foreign investment and advancing technology.

Pakistan's economic growth confronts several obstacles despite its potential. Income inequality, unemployment, and poverty are ongoing problems that need to be addressed. To address these issues, the government has started social assistance programs and programs to reduce poverty. To attract investments and promote economic development, it is crucial to improve the business climate, the infrastructure, and the economy.

As a whole, Pakistan is a dynamic and diversified country with a complicated political system, a growing economy, and a rich cultural legacy. Its topographical characteristics, which range from imposing mountains to riparian plains and deserts, contribute to its natural beauty and resource richness. Ancient civilizations, Islamic influences, and the effects of Mughal rule are all present in the history of the nation. With their friendliness, variety, and a strong feeling of belonging, Pakistanis contribute to the country's cultural diversity. Despite being hampered by moments of unrest, Pakistan's democratic government works to further equality and growth. As the nation strives for sustainable growth and the prosperity of its citizens, the economy—which is fueled by agriculture, industry, and services—presents both possibilities and problems.

Chapter 1: Preparing For Your Trip

Travel Documents and Visa Requirements

It is crucial to check that you have all the required travel papers and satisfy the visa requirements for your destination before making travel plans. You need to be informed of the particular visa and travel document requirements for Pakistan.

1. Passport: A passport that is currently valid is a need for travel. Make sure your passport is still valid for at least six months after the duration of your anticipated stay in Pakistan. To be safe, it is advised that you create a photocopy of your passport and store it separately.

2. Visa: The majority of travelers to Pakistan need a visa to enter the nation. Depending on your nationality, you may be able to secure a visa from a Pakistani embassy or consulate upon arrival or you might need to do so in advance. To get accurate and current information regarding visa requirements and application processes, it is advised to visit the official website of the Pakistani embassy or consulate in your home country.

3. Travel insurance: Having travel insurance that covers medical emergencies, trip cancellation or interruption, and lost or stolen possessions is strongly advised. Check your insurance to make sure it covers the demands and activities you'll be engaging in during your trip to Pakistan.

Safety and Health Advice

When going somewhere, health and safety need to come first. The following are important suggestions to bear in mind both before and during your visit to Pakistan:

1. Immunizations: To identify the required immunizations and preventive drugs, it is advised to see a healthcare provider or travel clinic before coming to Pakistan. Hepatitis A and B, typhoid, polio, tetanus, and diphtheria immunizations are often advised for Pakistan. Additional immunizations could be advised based on your travel intentions and medical background.

2. Medical Facilities: Get to know the hospitals and clinics in the Pakistani regions you want to visit. While hospitals and medical facilities in big cities are well-equipped, medical care in distant places may be scarce. Carry

a first-aid kit that has the necessities for treating minor ailments and wounds.

3. Food and Water Safety: Take measures to ensure the safety of your food and water to prevent stomach problems. Only water that has been adequately treated or boiled should be consumed. Street food, unpeeled fruits and vegetables, and raw or undercooked food should all be avoided unless they have been well-cleaned with clean water or peeled by you.

4. Personal Safety: Pakistan is typically a safe country to visit, but tourists should still use care and good judgment. Keep up with the latest security developments and heed any travel advice provided by your home country. Be aware of your surroundings, keep expensive objects

hidden, and take the required security measures to protect your property. To have a happy and courteous travel experience, observe the regional traditions and customs.

Important Items To Pack

Your vacation experience in Pakistan will be substantially improved if you bring the appropriate items. You should think about including the following goods on your packing list:

1. Pack clothes that are appropriate for the climate and cultural customs of the places you want to visit. Pakistan has a variety of climates, so it's a good idea to bring light, breathable clothes for the hot summers as well as layers that will keep you warm in the nights and throughout the winter, particularly in the northern areas. Pack modest clothes that cover your

knees and shoulders, especially if you want to visit religious places.

2. Footwear that is at ease: Pakistan provides options for both indoor and outdoor exploration. If you want to tour the mountainous areas, bring robust footwear for climbing or trekking in addition to comfortable walking shoes or sandals for city sightseeing.

3. Pakistan employs a three-pin plug system and operates at a voltage of 220-240V. A universal travel adapter could be useful to guarantee compatibility with local power outlets.

4. A lightweight travel towel, a reusable water bottle, a daypack for taking necessities on day excursions, a travel lock for locking your baggage, and a travel-sized umbrella or raincoat for

unforeseen weather changes are other helpful things to think about bringing.

Exchange Rates and Money

The Pakistani Rupee (PKR) is the country's official currency. Before your trip, it is a good idea to get acquainted with the current exchange rates and have a fundamental grasp of the local monetary system. The following advice is about money and trade in Pakistan:

1. Currency Exchange: In large cities, banks, and authorized exchange offices all provide a variety of currency exchange services. To guarantee fair exchange rates and prevent fake money, it is advised to exchange your currency at these approved locations.

2. Credit Cards and ATMs: Major credit cards are accepted at hotels, restaurants, and other bigger facilities, and ATMs are often accessible in

metropolitan areas. In contrast, it is advised to have enough cash on hand for smaller shops and distant locations where card acceptance can be scarce. To prevent any problems with card transactions, let your bank or credit card issuer know about your vacation intentions.

3. Carrying Cash: While having some cash on hand is vital, it is best to avoid carrying too much cash. To keep your cash and critical travel papers safe, use a money belt or a secure travel wallet.

Access To The Internet And Communication

Having access to the internet and staying connected may make traveling in Pakistan much easier. Here are several alternatives for connecting to the internet and communicating:

1. Mobile Networks: Upon arriving in Pakistan, you may buy a local SIM card from one of the country's well-established mobile network providers. This enables you to access data services while traveling, make local calls, and send text messages. Make sure your smartphone is unlocked and appropriate for the regional network frequencies.

2. Internet accessibility: In large cities, the majority of hotels, cafés, and restaurants provide free Wi-Fi to patrons. However, isolated locations could have slower or less reliable internet access. Before your journey, think about installing offline maps, applications for translating languages, and any other essential travel apps to make sure you have access to crucial information even without an internet connection.

3. Urban regions have access to public phones, and you may buy calling cards with pre-paid rates to make local and international calls. Convenience shops, kiosks, and a few mobile network providers sell these cards.

4. Use communication applications like WhatsApp, Skype, or Viber to make calls and send messages while connected to Wi-Fi or a data network. These applications might help connect with local acquaintances or keep in touch with relatives and friends back home.

To sum up, careful planning is essential for a hassle-free and pleasurable vacation to Pakistan. Make sure you have the required travel papers and visas, observe all necessary health and safety measures, pack just what you need, be acquainted with the local currency and exchange rates, and have a communication and internet connection plan in place. You may maximize your vacation to this culturally varied and wealthy nation by following these guidelines.

Chapter 2: How To Reach Pakistan

Airlines and Airports

Given Pakistan's international accessibility and the existence of several airports around the nation, air travel is the most popular and practical method of getting there. When arranging a flight to Pakistan, keep the following things in mind:

Major Airports: Pakistan has several international airports, with Jinnah International Airport in Karachi, Allama Iqbal International Airport in Lahore, and Islamabad International Airport in Islamabad serving as the country's three primary airports. Numerous airlines provide frequent flights to and from Pakistan from these airports, which have good connections to major cities all over the globe.

International Airlines: Several international airlines fly to Pakistan, giving passengers a variety of alternatives. Pakistan International Carriers (PIA), Emirates, Etihad Airways, Qatar Airways, Turkish Airlines, British Airways, and Air France are just a few of the well-known carriers that fly to Pakistan. It is wise to research prices, flight times, and other services provided by many airlines before selecting the one that best suits your travel requirements.

Connection Flights: You may need to take connecting flights to go to Pakistan, depending on your location and the airline you pick. For connecting flights to Pakistan, major international airports including Dubai, Abu Dhabi, Doha, Istanbul, and London often serve as the first stop. To prevent any difficulty, make sure you have enough time between flights for layovers.

Domestic flights are a practical choice if you want to go to many locations in Pakistan. To make it simpler to travel across the nation, several domestic airlines, notably PIA, Air Blue, and Serene Air provide flights between important cities. When traveling great distances, such as from Karachi to Lahore or Islamabad to Gilgit, domestic planes are very useful.

Border Crossings on Land

Land border crossings provide an alternate way for visitors from nearby nations to enter Pakistan. Here are some crucial considerations for land border crossings:

- The border between India and Pakistan: This is a crucial land crossing point for the two nations. However, the land border between India and Pakistan is strictly controlled, and entrance restrictions are in place owing to political unrest and security concerns. The

Wagah-Attari border, which is close to Lahore and Amritsar, is the sole legal crossing point for travelers. Before contemplating a land border crossing between India and Pakistan, it is crucial to confirm the most recent visa and entrance requirements as well as the security situation.

- The border between Afghanistan and Pakistan: This is another land crossing location, however, it is also subject to security restrictions. Torkham in Khyber Pakhtunkhwa province and Chaman in Balochistan province are the main border crossings. However, it is advised to take caution and carefully assess the present circumstances before contemplating a land border crossing from Afghanistan to Pakistan owing to the continuing war and security difficulties in Afghanistan.

- The border between Iran and Pakistan: Taftan acts as a gateway for people to go between the two nations and is accessible to travelers. Before arranging a land border crossing between Iran and Pakistan, it is advised to confirm the most recent visa requirements and security measures.

Ferries and Sea Ports

There are chances for maritime travel along Pakistan's coastline that borders the Arabian Maritime. Although arriving in Pakistan via water is less popular than by air, it is nevertheless feasible to do so through seaports and ferries. Here are some important things to think about:

Karachi Port: Karachi Port, which handles both freight and passenger boats, is Pakistan's biggest and busiest port. It links Pakistan to several foreign locations and acts as a significant marine commercial center. However, there are just a few varying passenger ferry services to Karachi.

Gwadar Port: The deep-sea port of Gwadar, which is situated in the Balochistan region, has grown in prominence recently as a result of its strategic position and the expansion of the China-Pakistan Economic Corridor (CPEC). While Gwadar Port focuses largely on business operations, it is anticipated that it would eventually play an important role in boosting regional connections and maybe luring passenger ferry services.

Cruise Ships: Pakistan is one of the ports where certain international cruise ships visit. These cruise ships provide the chance to go to places like Karachi, Gwadar, or the adjacent coastal regions. The availability and timetable of cruises to Pakistan should be specifically confirmed with cruise companies.

In conclusion, there are numerous ways to get to Pakistan, including flying into one of the nation's major airports, traveling across land borders from nearby nations (subject to security requirements and visa requirements), and possibly traveling by sea through ports like Karachi and Gwadar. To ensure a smooth and comfortable trip to Pakistan, it is important to plan your trip, taking into account variables like visa requirements, airline availability, security threats, and available modes of transportation.

Chapter 3: Exploring the Pakistani Regions

Pakistan is a nation of varied topography, rich cultural history, and energetic cities. From the throbbing center to the tranquil highland areas, each place gives guests a distinctive experience.

Capital Territory of Islamabad

Let's start our adventure in Islamabad, Pakistan's capital and the country's administrative and political hub. The well-designed infrastructure, rich vegetation, and scenic splendor of Islamabad are well-known. It is the perfect location for tourists since it provides a blend of contemporary amenities and natural attractions.

The Faisal Mosque, one of the biggest mosques in the world, is a famous landmark in Islamabad. It has a distinctive architecture that was modeled by a Bedouin tent in the desert. The mosque, which is at the base of the Margalla Hills, has a peaceful, meditative atmosphere.

Speaking about the Margalla Hills, they provide many chances for outdoor pursuits including hiking, trekking, and rock climbing and encircle Islamabad. The Margalla Hills is a well-liked destination for outdoor enthusiasts and wildlife lovers since the paths there provide beautiful views of the city and its surroundings.

Another must-see site in Islamabad is Daman-e-Koh. It is a viewpoint that provides a wide-angle view of the city and is located in the Margalla Hills. Visitors may take a leisurely walk around the city, have a picnic, or just sit back and admire

Islamabad's skyline, particularly after dusk when the city is bathed in a warm glow.

Rawal Lake is the ideal location for those looking for a peaceful escape. This man-made lake is situated on the outskirts of Islamabad and provides chances for boating, fishing, and picnics. It is surrounded by beautiful vegetation. It is the perfect location to get away from the bustle of the city and reconnect with nature.

Punjab Province

Moving on, we find ourselves in Punjab, Pakistan's most populated province, which is a place rich in history, cultural value, and agricultural importance. Punjab is a must-visit location for tourists because of its energetic cities, historical sites, and kind people.

The cultural center of Pakistan, Lahore, is a city rich in culture and history. It is renowned for its Mughal-era architecture, which includes Lahore Fort and Shalimar Gardens, both of which are UNESCO World Heritage Sites. The majestic Lahore Fort, also called Shahi Qila, was built during the Mughal Empire. The Sheesh Mahal (Palace of Mirrors), Diwan-e-Khas (Hall of Private Audience), and Naulakha Pavilion, among other elaborate architectural features, display the grandeur of the Mughal Empire.

The Badshahi Mosque, one of the biggest mosques in the world, is another architectural wonder in Lahore. It is a remarkable edifice with delicate marble inlay work and lovely calligraphy that was built by Emperor Aurangzeb. Thousands of worshipers may congregate in the mosque's expansive courtyard, and its minarets provide a sweeping perspective of the city.

It is pleasant to stroll around Lahore's bustling bazaars. The lively Anarkali Bazaar is famed for its traditional handicrafts, textiles, jewelry, and street food. It is named after a prostitute from the Mughal Empire. A broad range of regional specialties, including Lahori Chana Chaat, Seekh Kebabs, and Falooda, are offered on The Food Street in the old Walled City of Lahore.

Moving south, the "City of Saints," Multan, is renowned for its historic Sufi shrines and Sufi culture. Bahauddin Zakariya and Shah Rukn-e-Alam's mausoleums are important spiritual sites in the city. These temples draw both visitors and believers because of their elaborate architectural designs, vibrant tiles, and serene atmosphere.

The city of Taxila is a must-see for history buffs. Taxila is an archaeological site that displays the sophisticated Gandhara culture and is close to Islamabad. Ancient Buddhist colleges, stupas, and monasteries that are now in ruins may be visited to learn more about the history of the area and how Buddhism was influenced by it.

Visitors may experience the distinctive desert way of life by traveling into the Cholistan Desert, which is situated in the southern part of Punjab. Traditional desert towns may be found throughout the desert, and the residents there are kind and welcoming to visitors. A well-liked activity is camel safaris, which let tourists explore a huge area of golden dunes and take in the serenity of the desert. Motorsport fans from all over the globe go to Cholistan for the exhilarating annual Desert Rally.

Sindh Province

As we travel south, we reach Sindh, a region renowned for its thriving culture, historical attractions, and scenic coastline. In addition to vibrant cities, historic archeological sites, and tranquil seaside regions, Sindh has a rich history dating back to the Indus Valley civilization.

PAKISTAN TRAVEL GUIDE 2023

The biggest metropolis in Pakistan, Karachi, is a fusion of several cultures and provides a vivacious urban experience. The National Museum of Pakistan, which has a sizable collection of historical relics, Islamic works of art, and ethnographic displays, is one of the city's many tourist attractions. The beautiful Mohatta Palace, a building constructed in the early 20th century, is a prime example of how Indo-Islamic and European architectural styles may coexist together. The palace presently functions as a museum and gallery where exhibits and other cultural activities are held.

The southern region of Karachi's Clifton Beach is a well-liked destination for both residents and visitors to unwind and take in the Arabian Sea. The beach provides horseback riding and camel rides, and in the evenings, when food stands and entertainment options draw people of all ages, it comes to life.

The historic city of Thatta, a UNESCO World Heritage Site, is not far from Karachi. Thatta historically served as a significant hub for scholarship and commerce during the Mughal Empire. The Makli Necropolis, close to Thatta, is one of the world's biggest and most elaborately constructed funeral monuments. It has a large number of graves and mausoleums representing diverse historical eras and architectural styles.

A trip to the Mohenjo-daro ancient monument is essential for history aficionados. One of the world's earliest urban communities, the Indus Valley Civilization, left behind the archaeological wonder of Mohenjo-Daro. Insights about the architecture, urban design, and manner of life of the ancient city may be gained from the well-preserved remains.

A visit to the lovely Hingol National Park is strongly advised for those who like the outdoors. The biggest national park in

Pakistan is Hingol National Park, which is situated in the southern province of Sindh. The endangered Houbara Bustard and Marsh Crocodile are only two examples of the variety of species that may be found there. Nature lovers and explorers are drawn to the park's untamed wilderness, soaring cliffs, and breathtaking vistas.

Province of Khyber Pakhtunkhwa

We reach Khyber Pakhtunkhwa (KPK), a province renowned for its spectacular mountainous scenery, historical landmarks, and cultural diversity, as we go toward the northwest of Pakistan. The Hindu Kush and Karakoram mountain ranges' towering peaks may be found in KPK, where they provide beautiful vistas and thrilling experiences.

The dynamic city of Peshawar, which serves as KPK's capital, is home to a wide variety of cultural groups. The Qissa Khwani Bazaar, a part of the old city, is well-known for its traditional marketplaces, historic value, and old architecture. A sizable collection of Gandharan artworks, illustrating the area's Buddhist roots, may be seen at the Peshawar Museum.

The Swat Valley, sometimes known as the "Switzerland of Pakistan," is an attractive area noted for its verdant meadows, flowing rivers, and snow-capped hills. It provides chances for skiing, trekking, and visiting historic Buddhist sites like the Buddhist Stupas at Jahanabad.

A mountain route that links Pakistan and Afghanistan is known as the Khyber route. It has strategic and cultural significance and has been important in commerce and migration throughout history. Visitors may explore the past, discover its historical importance, and benefit from the friendliness of the locals.

The Chitral district's Kalash Valley is a special place with a distinctive culture, language, and religious traditions. The Kalash people, with their exuberant festivals, distinctive garb, and long-standing traditions, contribute to the allure of the valley. The valley's breathtaking scenery, which includes terraced crops and snow-capped summits, adds to the allure.

Balochistan Province

The biggest province of Pakistan, Balochistan, is a country of untamed scenery, historical attractions, and a rich cultural history. It is an area with enormous deserts, soaring mountains, and stunning coastlines.

Balochistan's main city, Quetta, is tucked away amid mountains and enjoys beautiful weather all year round. The endangered Markhor may be found in the Hazarganji

Chiltan National Park, which is not far from Quetta.

A large port and a vital point on the China-Pakistan Economic Corridor (CPEC), Gwadar is a coastal city in Balochistan. The stunning beaches, crystal-clear oceans, and coral reefs of Gwadar make it a growing tourist attraction. Visitors may engage in fishing, water sports, and unique marine life exploration.

Balochistan is also a part of the Hingol National Park, which was previously stated in the Sindh Province section. Nature lovers and thrill seekers are drawn to the park's varied scenery, which includes the well-known Princess of Hope rock formation and the Mud Volcanoes.

The hill station of Ziarat, which is situated in the Ziarat district, is well-known for its nice weather, juniper trees, and the former Quaid-e-Azam Residency. Muhammad Ali

Jinnah, the man who founded Pakistan, spent his last days at the Quaid-e-Azam Residency. It has historical value and has been conserved as a museum.

Region of Gilgit-Baltistan

Often referred to as the "roof of the world," Gilgit-Baltistan is a mountainous area in northeastern Pakistan. It is renowned for its stunning scenery, towering peaks, and extensive cultural history.

An entrance to the area is Gilgit, the capital of Gilgit-Baltistan. The city serves as a base for further exploration and provides breathtaking views of the Karakoram Range. The city's attractiveness is enhanced by the Gilgit River, which runs through it.

The Hunza Valley, located in the Karakoram Range, is well known for its breathtaking scenery, terraced crops, and friendly locals. The valley is home to ancient forts and traditional communities as well as stunning vistas of Rakaposhi, Diran Peak, and Ultar Peak. The region's colorful events, including the well-known Hunza Blossom Festival, highlight the rich cultural traditions of the local populace.

Adventure lovers love to go to Skardu, which is situated on the banks of the Indus River. also provides chances for climbing, hiking, and experiencing Balti culture, and also serves as the starting point for expeditions to the K2 summit, which is the second-highest mountain in the world. Must-see sights in the area include the gorgeous Satpara Lake and the Shigar Valley, which is famous for its historic forts and traditional architecture.

Fairy Meadows, an idyllic alpine meadow with breathtaking views of the surrounding peaks, is located at the foot of Nanga Parbat, one of the highest mountains in the world. It's a well-liked location for camping, hiking, and taking in the scenery. The Fairy

Meadows hike, which passes through deep woods and meadows filled with wildflowers, is a fascinating adventure.

Region of Azad Jammu and Kashmir

Azad Jammu and Kashmir (AJK), a province in northwest Pakistan that borders both India and the Jammu and Kashmir area that is controlled by India, is renowned for its natural beauty, verdant valleys, and historical landmarks.

The capital of AJK, Muzaffarabad, is perched on the banks of the Jhelum River and provides spectacular views of the mountains in the area. The Muzaffarabad Fort, commonly known as the Red Fort, serves as a reminder of the area's historical importance. Visitors may tour the fort's architectural features, go inside the museum, and take in the expansive city views.

The Neelum Valley is a lovely valley with thick woods, thundering waterfalls, and stunning vistas. It was called after the Neelum River. It provides a peaceful getaway and acts as a starting point for exploring the stunning valleys of AJK. The Neelum Valley's Athmuqam is a well-liked starting place for exploring the valley and its features.

The old Sharda University ruins are located in the historic town of Sharda in the AJK region. It is an important spiritual and educational location that draws academics and visitors curious about the area's historical past. The town's natural beauty is enhanced by its setting on the banks of the Neelum River.

The Mangla Dam, one of Pakistan's biggest dams, is situated on the Jhelum River. There are boating, fishing, and picnicking options in the reservoir that the dam creates. The vicinity is a sanctuary for birdwatchers as well since many different migrating bird species may be seen here.

In conclusion, tourists may enjoy a variety of experiences around Pakistan. Each area has its distinct appeal and charms, from the energetic metropolis of Islamabad, Lahore, and Karachi to the tranquil mountains of Gilgit-Baltistan and the ancient landmarks in Punjab and Sindh. Visitors may fully experience Pakistan's rich culture, natural beauty, and historical importance by exploring these areas. Pakistan has something to offer to any tourist looking for a special and unforgettable experience, whether they are interested in discovering old historical sites, hiking in the Karakoram Range, or enjoying the friendliness of the local population.

Chapter 4: Major Cities and Vacation Spots

Lahore

The city of Lahore, which is often referred to as Pakistan's cultural capital, is rich in culture, history, and architectural wonders. A rich fusion of Mughal, Sikh, and British colonial influences makes it an alluring tourist destination.

One of the city's must-see attractions is the Lahore Fort, which is a UNESCO World Heritage Site. Beautiful palaces, courtyards, and gardens can be seen within this huge stronghold that was constructed during the Mughal period. With its walls covered with beautiful mirror work, the well-known Sheesh Mahal, also known as the Palace of Mirrors, is a magnificent illustration of painstaking workmanship.

The magnificent Badshahi Mosque, one of the biggest mosques in the world, sits just next to the Lahore Fort. Visitors from all over the globe are drawn to it by its magnificent architecture, which is embellished with marble and red sandstone. Both worshipers and guests may find calm in the mosque's expansive courtyard and minarets.

One may tour the renowned Walled City of Lahore by meandering through the congested streets of the Old City. The brilliant colors, fragrant spices, and traditional handicrafts at the humming bazaars, like the Anarkali Bazaar, are a sensory feast. A hidden treasure worth exploring is the neighboring Wazir Khan Mosque, which is renowned for its beautiful tile work and paintings.

Lahore is recognized for having a thriving food scene. Foodies may savor the city's wonderful street cuisine, which includes spicily spiced kebabs, fragrant biryanis, and tempting sweets like falooda and jalebi. A well-liked location to indulge in these gastronomic treats is Food Street in the Old City.

Karachi

The biggest and most important city in Pakistan, Karachi, is a busy metropolis with a diverse population, cutting-edge buildings, and a breathtaking coastline. It provides a distinctive fusion of historical landmarks, busy marketplaces, and a vibrant urban environment.

A treasure trove of relics, illustrating the nation's rich history and varied cultural traditions, may be found at the National Museum of Pakistan in Karachi. It has a sizable collection of historical artifacts, Islamic art, and ethnographic displays that provide light on the area's history.

The southern region of Karachi's Clifton Beach is a well-liked destination for both residents and visitors to unwind and take in the Arabian Sea. The beach provides horseback riding and camel rides, and in the evenings, when food stands and entertainment options draw people of all ages, it comes to life.

Early 20th-century home Mohatta Palace is a superb example of Indo-Islamic and European architectural fusion. The palace presently functions as a museum and gallery where exhibits and other cultural activities are held.

The vibrant marketplaces of Karachi provide a broad variety of alternatives for shoppers. Fresh food, spices, and traditional handicrafts may be found in Empress Market, a famous shopping destination with architecture from the colonial past. For its chic boutiques, cafés, and designer shops, Defence Housing Authority's (DHA) upmarket neighborhood Zamzama Street is well-known.

Islamabad

The capital of Pakistan, Islamabad, is a contemporary, well-planned metropolis tucked away in the Margalla Hills. It serves as the nation's political and administrative hub and provides a serene atmosphere with its broad avenues, green areas, and breathtaking scenery.

One of the biggest mosques in the world, the Faisal Mosque, is a well-known landmark in Islamabad. It is stunning due to its distinctive style, which was influenced by traditional Islamic architecture, and it's setting against the Margalla Hills. Tens of thousands of worshipers may be accommodated in the mosque's spacious courtyard.

The Pakistan Monument, a representation of pride in one's country and solidarity, is located next to the Faisal Mosque. The monument, which is shaped like a flower in bloom, has beautiful stone sculptures that illustrate the history and culture of Pakistan's several regions.

On the outskirts of Islamabad, the Margalla Hills National Park provides chances for trekking, picnicking, and taking in the scenery. The park's pathways take you to beautiful lookout sites like Daman-e-Koh, which offers sweeping city vistas.

The Lok Virsa Museum, which is committed to conserving and advancing Pakistani culture, has a sizable collection of traditional musical instruments and arts and crafts. Through its exhibits and live performances, it provides visitors with an understanding of the various cultural legacy of the nation.

Peshawar

One of the oldest cities in South Asia is Peshawar, the provincial capital of Khyber

Pakhtunkhwa. It is renowned for its bazaars, historical landmarks, and thriving Pashtun culture. It has a long, rich history that dates back thousands of years.

History buffs should not miss a trip to the Peshawar Museum. It has a magnificent collection of Gandhara art, which was prevalent in the area in antiquity. Buddhist statues, antique coins, and other relics that provide light on the Gandhara civilization's aesthetic and cultural history are on display at the museum.

In Peshawar's Old City, a bustling bazaar called the Qissa Khwani Bazaar, popularly called the "Street of Storytellers," is located. It is renowned for its traditional bazaars, where one can get everything from handicrafts and jewelry to textiles and spices. The market is fascinating to visit because of its lively atmosphere and historical importance.

A reminder of Peshawar's historic past is the Bala Hisar Fort, which is positioned on a hill and offers views of the city. The fort has held government offices in addition to being a royal home and a military fortress. Visitors may tour the fort's architectural features, go inside the museum, and take in expansive city vistas.

The cuisine of Peshawar is a unique fusion of Central and South Asian cuisines with traditional Pashtun spices. Delicious delicacies like Chapli kebabs, Peshawari karahi, and classic desserts like Kheer and Gulab Jamun are available for foodies to enjoy. Locals and visitors congregate at the barbecue restaurants in the Namak Mandi region to savor succulent kebabs and grilled meats.

Quetta

The province of Balochistan's capital, Quetta, is renowned for its scenic beauty, untamed fields, and comfortable climate. It provides a unique fusion of natural marvels and cultural history and is surrounded by mountains.

A well-liked picnic area is Hanna Lake, which is a few kilometers from Quetta. It offers a tranquil retreat from the busy metropolis thanks to its turquoise waters and the surrounding nature. Boating on the lake, strolling along its promenade, and unwinding in the tranquil setting are all available to visitors.

On the outskirts of Quetta, the Hazarganji Chiltan National Park is a refuge for those who enjoy the outdoors. It is home to a variety of plants and animals, such as the uncommon Afghan Ural and the endangered Markhor. Hiking and animal viewing possibilities may be found throughout the park's picturesque pathways and vantage spots.

Traditional handicrafts from Quetta are also well-known, notably the elaborate Balochi carpets and needlework. These handicrafts, together with fresh food, spices, and regional attire, may be purchased in the crowded bazaars of Liaquat and Kandahari.

The adjoining hill station of Ziarat is home to the historical landmark known as the Quaid-e-Azam Residency. Quaid-e-Azam Muhammad Ali Jinnah, the founding father of Pakistan, spent his last days here. The residence is now a museum that keeps the memorabilia and antiques connected to Quaid-e-Azam.

Gilgit

The capital of the Gilgit-Baltistan province, Gilgit, is a gateway to the magnificent Karakoram Range and a starting point for treks and mountaineering excursions. It provides a sanctuary for nature lovers with its stunning mountain peaks, glaciers, and rivers all around.

Gilgit and China's Xinjiang province are connected by the Karakoram Highway, which is sometimes referred to as the "Eighth Wonder of the World." With its magnificent vistas, hairpin curves, and panoramic views of the Karakoram Range, this famous road trip is a delight for adventurers.

Traditional bazaars in Gilgit are humming hubs of activity where residents go to purchase and sell a range of goods. Visitors may discover distinctive handicrafts, gemstones, traditional apparel, and delectable regional food in the bustling Gilgit Main Bazaar.

A major historical and religious landmark close to Gilgit is the 7th-century rock sculpture of the Buddha known as Kargah Buddha. It draws tourists interested in archaeology and ancient cultures and is said to be a monument to the area's Buddhist legacy.

Hunza Valley

The Gilgit-Baltistan region's Hunza Valley is well known for its spectacular natural beauty, verdant valleys, and snow-capped mountains. It is sometimes referred to as "Heaven on Earth" and provides visitors with a peaceful respite.

Hunza's main village, Karimabad Village, is positioned atop a hill with a valley view. It provides sweeping views of the nearby peaks, such as Ladyfinger Peak, Rakaposhi, and Ultar. The village's well-known features include its old-fashioned stone homes, terraced fields, and bright apricot orchards.

A historical fort near Karimabad called the Baltit Fort is a UNESCO World Heritage Site. It highlights the region's traditional architecture and provides information about the history and culture of the surrounding areas. The museum in the fort displays objects and images that highlight the history of the area.

The magnificent turquoise Attabad Lake, also known as the Gojal Lake, was created by a landslide in 2010. It has grown to be a well-liked tourist destination, providing chances for boating and taking in the natural beauty of the mountains around.

In the spring, the Hunza Valley is renowned for its cherry blossoms. The valley is transformed into a lovely setting by the blossoming cherry trees, drawing tourists from all around. Another significant occasion that promotes the traditional game of polo and unites the regional people is the Shandur Polo Festival, which is annually in July.

Swat Valley

The Khyber Pakhtunkhwa province's Swat Valley is renowned for its verdant meadows, sparkling lakes, and snow-capped mountains. Due to its historical importance and natural beauty, it has long been a well-liked tourist attraction.

The Swat Museum is located in Mingora, the largest city in the Swat Valley, and it is home to a great collection of Gandhara relics. Buddhist statues, old coins, and artifacts from other cultures are displayed at the museum to show the diverse cultural legacy of the area.

Adventure seekers go to Malam Jabba, a well-known ski resort in Swat Valley, throughout the winter. It provides chairlifts, skiing slopes, and spectacular views of the mountains around. Malam Jabba becomes a gorgeous hideaway in the summer, complete with verdant meadows and vibrant alpine flowers.

A haven for those who enjoy the outdoors is the Kalam Valley, which is situated near

Swat at a higher elevation. It is well-known for its beautiful scenery, waterfalls, and streams that are stocked with trout. While taking in the calm beauty of the valley, visitors may engage in activities like hiking, camping, and trout fishing.

Several historic Buddhist monuments, including the Butkara and Shingardar stupas, can be found in the Swat Valley. Scholars and history buffs visit these archeological sites, which represent the area's strong Buddhist legacy.

Murree

The Punjab hill station of Murree is a well-liked summer getaway because of its comfortable climate and breathtaking scenery. It provides a cool respite from the heat of the plains and draws visitors with its verdant green trees, undulating hills, and colonial-era buildings.

The Mall Road, Murree's main street, is lined with stores, eateries, and cafés. Visitors may take a walk down the road while taking in the refreshing mountain air and perusing a selection of locally-made crafts, apparel, and mementos.

Near Murree, there is a thrilling ride that gives sweeping views of the hills and valleys around called the Patriata Chairlift. Visitors may enjoy a bird's-eye view of the scenic setting from the summit of New Murree, where they are transported by chairlift.

Ayubia National Park is a protected region close to Murree that is well-known for its hiking routes and wildlife. It provides possibilities for peaceful outdoor activities including picnics, birding, and nature hikes.

Multan

Multan, sometimes referred to as the "City of Sufis," is one of the oldest towns in South Asia and is significant both historically and religiously. It is situated in the region of Punjab and is renowned for its magnificent architectural works, Sufi shrines, and lively culture.

The magnificent historical landmark known as the Multan Fort, or Qila Multan, has seen the rise and fall of several civilizations. The fort's stunning architecture, especially it's elaborate gates and high walls, displays the long history of the area. The shrine of the famed Sufi saint Bahauddin Zakariya is also located within the fort.

Another notable Sufi shrine in Multan, the Mausoleum of Shah Rukn-e-Alam, is an architectural marvel. It draws believers and tourists looking for spiritual peace since it is devoted to the Sufi saint Shah Rukn-e-Alam.

Multan is well known for its thriving bazaars, where one can take in the energetic atmosphere of the city and locate a wide selection of traditional handicrafts. A well-liked bazaar called the Hussain Agahi Bazaar is well-known for its vibrant fabrics, ceramics, and delicately crafted Multani blue pottery.

Faisalabad

The industrial city of Faisalabad, commonly referred to as the "Manchester of Pakistan," is located in the Punjab region. It is a significant hub for commerce, industry, and textiles and provides a distinctive fusion of contemporary architecture and old sites.

On the outskirts of Faisalabad, there is a refuge for several animal and bird species called Gatwala Wildlife Park. It offers peaceful chances for picnics, nature walks enjoyment, and animal viewing.

In the center of Faisalabad, the Clock Tower serves as a representation of the city's character. It is a well-known sight that attracts both residents and tourists and is surrounded by vibrant marketplaces. The nearby bazaars provide an exciting shopping experience with a variety of fabrics, apparel, and handicrafts.

The Lyallpur Museum, which bears the city's original name, offers information on the past, present, and future of Faisalabad. It displays historical relics, images, and records, including information on the region's importance to the textile industry.

Rawalpindi

The busy city of Rawalpindi, which is close to Islamabad, has a significant historical and cultural past. It provides a mix of modernism and traditional charm and acts as a gateway to Pakistan's northern areas.

The Rawalpindi Museum, sometimes called the Army Museum, presents Pakistan's military history. It features an extensive collection of items from the nation's military services, including relics, gear, uniforms, and souvenirs.

One of Rawalpindi's biggest and oldest marketplaces, Raja Bazaar, is a bustling place to shop. It provides a variety of products, such as clothing, jewelry, handicrafts, and regional foods. Visitors may fully immerse themselves in the energetic environment and learn about the local culture.

Several historical locations, including the Taxila archaeological sites and the Rawat Fort, can be found in Rawalpindi. These locations serve as reminders of the area's ancient past and attract tourists interested in history and archaeology.

The Lok Virsa Legacy Museum in Rawalpindi displays traditional clothing, musical instruments, and folk art to highlight the rich cultural legacy of Pakistan. It offers tourists a look at the vibrant cultural variety of the nation.

To sum up, Pakistan is a lucky nation with a wide variety of important cities and tourist attractions. Each place provides a distinctive experience, from the ancient sites in Lahore to the throbbing city of Karachi, from Islamabad's serene beauty to Peshawar's and Quetta's rocky vistas and the breathtaking valleys of Gilgit, Hunza, and Swat. Every tourist can find something to do in Pakistan, whether they like to take in the country's natural marvels, explore historical civilizations, indulge in local cuisine, or explore colorful bazaars.

Chapter 5: Cultural and Historical Places

With a wide variety of historical landmarks that highlight its ancient civilizations, architectural marvels, and religious legacy, Pakistan is a nation rich in history and culture. Pakistan provides a wealth of experiences for history buffs and cultural connoisseurs, including UNESCO World Heritage Sites, archaeological remains, forts and palaces, mosques and shrines, museums and art galleries, and bustling cultural festivals.

UNESCO World Heritage Sites

Several UNESCO World Heritage Sites that have been honored for their exceptional global worth may be found in Pakistan. These locations provide visitors with a look at the rich historical and cultural history of the nation.

The Archaeological Ruins at Mohenjo Daro are one of Pakistan's most well-known UNESCO sites. Mohenjo Daro is a historic city from the third millennium BCE that is situated in the Sindh province. The location exhibits the ruins of one of the first urban communities in history, together with many well-preserved buildings, including the Great Bath, granaries, and houses. Mohenjo Daro's elaborate urban design and cutting-edge engineering provide important new perspectives on the Indus Valley Civilization.

Another UNESCO World Heritage Site is the Buddhist Ruins of Takht-i-Bahi and Sahr-i-Bahlol, which are close to Mardan in the province of Khyber Pakhtunkhwa. These prehistoric ruins, which date to the first century BCE, include the wreckage of Buddhist monastic structures, stupas, and artwork. They emphasize the development of early Buddhist art and architecture as well as Buddhism's effect on the area.

Lahore's Shalimar Gardens and Lahore Fort are both included as UNESCO World Heritage Sites. A spectacular fortification from the Mughal period, the Lahore Fort exhibits a synthesis of Islamic, Persian, and Hindu architectural traditions. The Sheesh Mahal (Palace of Mirrors) and the Diwan-e-Khas (Hall of Special Audience) are two of its prominent buildings. The Shalimar Gardens, which were constructed under Emperor Shah Jahan and include terraces, fountains, and pavilions, is a magnificent illustration of Mughal garden architecture.

Another UNESCO property that goes back to the 16th century is the Rohtas Fort, which is located close to Jhelum in the Punjab state. Sher Shah Suri constructed this massive structure, which functioned as a strategic stronghold. Its sturdy construction and defensive characteristics are evidence of the era's military might.

The Makli Necropolis is a sizable burial complex that occupies an area of around 10 square kilometers close to the city of Thatta in the Sindh province. Numerous mausoleums and graves of different architectural styles from the 14th to the 18th century may be seen there. The Makli Necropolis is a representation of the regional aesthetic and cultural heritage.

Archeological Ruins

Numerous archeological sites in Pakistan provide information about its historical eras and ancient civilizations. The vast and varied cultural legacy of the nation is attested to by these ruins.

Taxila, a historic city close to Islamabad, is a treasure trove of archeological finds. It served as a significant center for Buddhist education as well as a crossroads for trade and commerce along the Silk Road. The Taxila ruins include the remnants of Buddhist temples, stupas, and other buildings that demonstrate the area's connection to Buddhism.

Ancient archaeological sites from the Indus Valley Civilization may be found in Pakistan at Harappa and Mohenjo-Daro. These locations, which date to the third millennium BCE, are among the earliest urban communities in the world. The Indus Valley Civilization's advanced urban planning, drainage systems, and creative activities are seen in the ruins of Harappa and Mohenjo-Daro.

Another significant archeological site is the ancient city of Uch Sharif, which may be found in the Punjab province's Bahawalpur district. Several antique mosques, tombs, and mausoleums may be found there, and it formerly served as a significant cultural and intellectual hub throughout the Middle Ages. The elaborate tile work and architectural aspects of the buildings are a reflection of the period's creative heritage.

Palaces and Forts

The rich history and regal legacy of Pakistan are reflected in the forts and palaces that make up its architectural heritage. The architecture of these buildings combines Islamic, Persian, Mughal, and native architectural traditions.

One of the finest examples of a beautiful Mughal fortification is the Lahore Fort, which was previously named a UNESCO World Heritage Site. In the center of Lahore, it stands erect, showcasing amazing architectural elements and including several palaces, gardens, and museums.

The previously stated powerful structure of Rohtas Fort was crucial in the history of the area. Its substantial gates, walls, and bastions provide evidence of its defensive importance.

The Red Fort, a medieval fort in Muzaffarabad, Azad Jammu, and Kashmir, is well-known for its breathtaking setting with a view of the Neelum River. It was first erected in the 16th century by the Chak kings, and the Mughals subsequently rebuilt it. The fort provides sweeping views of the city and the mountains around it.

An amazing desert stronghold may be seen in Punjab province's Cholistan Desert at the Derawar Fort. A local Rajput prince constructed it in the ninth century, and several dynasties afterward took control of it. In the desolate setting, the fort's enormous walls and towering bastions are a captivating sight.

The Hiran Minar is a distinctive structure created by Emperor Jahangir and is located in Sheikhupura, Punjab. It gives a panoramic view of the surrounding landscape and has a tall tower decorated with stone antelope heads.

Shrines and Mosques

Pakistan, a nation with a large Muslim population, is home to several mosques and shrines of important historical and religious importance. These architectural wonders are significant pilgrimage destinations and display a range of Islamic architectural styles.

One of Pakistan's biggest and most recognizable mosques is the Badshahi Mosque in Lahore. It is a masterwork of Mughal architecture, including imposing domes, minarets, and dexterous marble work. It was constructed during the Mughal period. The mosque is renowned for its breathtaking beauty and can hold more than 100,000 worshipers.

The Faisal Mosque in Islamabad is a stunning example of contemporary architecture. It is one of the biggest mosques in the world and the biggest in Pakistan. It was created by a Turkish architect and mixes modern and conventional Islamic architecture. The distinctive architecture of the mosque, with its modern lines and remarkable geometry, has come to represent Islamabad.

Lahore's Shrine of Data Ganj Bakhsh is a respected Sufi shrine and a popular destination for pilgrims. The Sufi saint Hazrat Ali Hajveri, also known as Data Ganj Bakhsh, is buried there. Those seeking spiritual consolation are drawn to the shrine's exquisite architecture, which is embellished with marble and colorful tile work.

Another famous Sufi shrine is the Shrine of Lal Shahbaz Qalandar, which is located in Sehwan Sharif, Sindh province. It is recognized for its lively atmosphere and devotional ceremonies and is devoted to the Sufi saint Lal Shahbaz Qalandar. A special spiritual atmosphere is produced by the shrine's remarkable design and the pulsating Sufi music performed throughout the meetings.

The Shahi Eidgah Mosque in Multan is a historic building renowned for its exquisite blue tile work and deft calligraphy. It was constructed under the rule of the Delhi Sultanate and is regarded as a jewel of local architecture.

Museums and Art Galleries

Numerous museums and galleries that conserve and present the history, art, and cultural legacy of Pakistan may be found there. These establishments provide a wealth of information and a window into the many dimensions of Pakistan's cultural character.

The biggest museum in Pakistan is the National Museum, which is situated in Karachi. It has a sizable collection of antiquities, works of art, and historical items that illustrate Pakistan's history, culture, and archaeology. Ancient Indus Valley Civilization relics, Islamic artwork and calligraphy, ethnographic exhibitions, and modern art are all on show at the museum.

One of the first museums established in Pakistan is the Lahore Museum, which is located in Lahore. Its collection of items is vast and includes Gandhara sculptures, antiquities from the Mughal and Sikh eras, miniature paintings, and Islamic artwork. The museum's vast collection provides a thorough overview of the history and creative traditions of the area.

The Mohatta Palace Museum is situated in a magnificent palace that was constructed during the British Raj and is located in

Karachi. Through its textile, pottery, sculpture, and painting displays, the museum presents Pakistan's aesthetic and cultural legacy. The museum's appeal is heightened by the palace's exquisite architecture and lovely grounds.

The Lok Virsa Museum, as was previously mentioned, is a cultural institution in Islamabad that celebrates the rich history of Pakistan. It has an extensive collection of folk art, crafts, traditional clothing, musical instruments, and antiques from many parts of the nation. The museum also presents cultural activities and performances, giving guests a comprehensive view of Pakistan's diverse cultural heritage.

Events and Festivals of Culture

Pakistan is renowned for its lively cultural celebrations and events that highlight the nation's many cultures, traditions, and creative manifestations. These celebrations provide a special chance to take in traditional music, dancing, cuisine, and cultural acts.

Springtime is heralded by the Basant Festival, which is observed in Lahore and other areas of Punjab province. It is renowned for hosting exciting kite-flying contests and showcasing traditional music and dance. The city comes to life as bright kites fly through the sky, and happiness and excitement permeate the air.

An annual Sufi event known as the Urs of Data Ganj Bakhsh is conducted at the Data Darbar shrine in Lahore. It honors the Sufi saint's death anniversary and draws followers from all around the nation. The celebration is distinguished by Sufi Qawwali performances, devotional music, and a vibrant spiritual atmosphere.

A distinctive cultural occasion that highlights the customs and ceremonies of the Kalash people is the Kalash Festival, which takes place in the Kalash Valley in Chitral. The celebration offers a glimpse into the local indigenous culture and traditions via colorful dances, lively music, and traditional attire.

A spectacular sports occasion, the Shandur Polo Festival draws polo fans from all over the globe to the Shandur Pass in Gilgit-Baltistan. The "highest polo ground in the world" is renowned for providing a one-of-a-kind chance to see polo matches among stunning mountain views.

The Sibi Mela is a historic agricultural fair that has been held in Sibi, Balochistan province, for more than a thousand years. Through camel racing, ethnic dances, artisan displays, and traditional music performances, it highlights Balochistan's cultural legacy.

In conclusion, visiting Pakistan's historical and cultural places is a wonderful way to learn about the history of the nation. These locations, which include forts, palaces, mosques, and shrines in addition to UNESCO World Heritage Sites and archeological remains, provide important insights into Pakistan's historical civilizations, architectural marvels, and religious traditions. Intense festivals and events honor Pakistan's customs, music, dance, and food, while museums and art galleries preserve and present the nation's many cultural manifestations. Visitors may get fully immersed in the fascinating fabric of Pakistan's history and culture by seeing these locations and taking part in the local festivals.

Chapter 6: Natural Wonders and Outdoor Adventures

Pakistan is endowed with a variety of scenery, including imposing mountains, rough terrain, tranquil lakes, raging rivers, immaculate beaches, immense deserts, and enchanted woods. Outdoor enthusiasts have a playground in these natural beauties, which also provide a wide range of adventurous activities and chances to discover the amazing beauty of the nation. Pakistan is a haven for nature lovers and adventure seekers, offering everything from climbing and trekking in the mountains to visiting national parks, taking part in water sports, and finding secret caverns.

Trekking & Hiking

Himalayan, Karakoram, and Hindu Kush mountain ranges are just a few of Pakistan's breathtaking mountain ranges. For travelers of all skill levels, these mountains provide fantastic climbing and trekking options. There are paths and routes for every interest and ability level, whether you're a seasoned climber or a newbie hiker.

The Karakoram Highway is a well-liked route for car excursions and hiking expeditions. It is sometimes referred to as the "Eighth Wonder of the World." It extends from Islamabad to the highest paved international border crossing in the world, the Khunjerab Pass. Trekkers may take in the beautiful scenery along the journey, which includes the famous Karakoram Range and the lovely Hunza Valley.

For seasoned hikers, the Nanga Parbat Base Camp Trek is a difficult yet rewarding excursion. Nanga Parbat, sometimes referred to as the "Killer Mountain," is the ninth-highest mountain on Earth. The walk provides breathtaking views of the mountain and its glaciers as well as the chance to fully experience the Balti people's indigenous culture.

One of the most well-known and difficult treks in the world is the K2 Base Camp Trek. Mountaineering legend K2 is the second-highest peak in the world. The Baltoro Glacier and Concordia, a spectacular confluence of several glaciers encircled by towering peaks, are just two of the beautiful vistas you'll pass through on the walk.

The Fairy Meadows and Nanga Parbat Viewpoint Trek is a fantastic option for those looking for a more leisurely trekking experience. The walk, which is in the Gilgit-Baltistan area, passes through verdant meadows, pine woods, and charming villages while providing breathtaking views of Nanga Parbat.

Climbing and Mountaineering

Climbers from all over the globe go to Pakistan in search of the country's formidable peaks since it is a mountaineer's paradise. Five of the top 14 mountains in the world are found in this region: K2, Broad Peak, Gasherbrum I, Gasherbrum II, and Nanga Parbat.

The "Savage Mountain," or K2, is the gem in Pakistan's mountain crown. It is known for its technical difficulties and severe weather since it is the second-highest mountain in the globe. It takes tremendous mountaineering expertise, experience, and physical endurance to complete the mammoth task of climbing K2.

Another dangerous mountain, Nanga Parbat, sometimes known as the "Killer Mountain," has taken the lives of several climbers. Due to its dangerous terrain, incline, and unpredictable weather, it poses considerable difficulties. In the realm of climbing, successfully reaching Nanga Parbat's peak is regarded as an incredible accomplishment.

Rock climbers from all over the world come to the Trango Towers, a series of granite spires in the Karakoram Range. For climbers of all ability levels, these vertical rock formations provide a range of difficult routes.

Wildlife Refuges And National Parks

Numerous national parks and wildlife sanctuaries may be found in Pakistan, conserving the country's unique biodiversity and providing a habitat for a diverse variety of plants and animals. These protected areas provide chances for animal viewing, birding, nature hikes, and camping in the middle of breathtaking scenery.

The biggest national park in Pakistan is called Hingol National Park, and it is situated in the Balochistan province. It is renowned for having a variety of scenery, including rocky mountains, mud volcanoes, dunes, and coastal regions. The endangered Balochistan bear, Ibex, and chinkara are just a few of the many animal species that call the park home.

The "Roof of the World," also known as Deosai National Park, is situated in Gilgit-Baltistan. It is one of the world's highest plateaus, and in the summer, it is covered with a stunning carpet of wildflowers. The endangered and uncommon Himalayan brown bear is another animal that may be seen in Deosai.

The Karakoram Range's Khunjerab National Park is renowned for its breathtaking vistas and diverse wildlife. The park is home to several different bird species, including the famous Marco Polo sheep, Himalayan ibex, and snow leopards. The park's entrance is the aforementioned Khunjerab Pass, which also provides beautiful views of the mountains around.

Near Islamabad, the Margalla Hills National Park is a well-liked spot for hiking, birdwatching, and nature walks. The park's verdant hills, trees, and trails provide a tranquil haven from the bustle of the city.

Lakes and Rivers

Pakistan is endowed with a large number of lakes and rivers, which provide chances for leisure, adventure, and water sports. These bodies of water are surrounded by stunning scenery, making them well-liked tourist attractions.

One of the most stunning lakes in Pakistan is Lake Saiful Muluk, which is found in the Kaghan Valley in Khyber Pakhtunkhwa. It is renowned for its turquoise waters and is tucked away among snow-capped mountains. The lake has boating and camping amenities, and it is bordered by lovely hiking routes.

Gilgit-Baltistan's Lake Attabad sometimes referred to as the "Hunza Lake," is a magnificent turquoise body of water. It was created by a significant landslide and is encircled by imposing mountains. The lake is a favorite place for boating and provides expansive views of the surroundings.

The biggest freshwater lake in Pakistan is Manchar Lake, which is located in Sindh province. It is renowned for having a wide range of fish species and migratory bird species. The lake provides chances for fishing and boating and is a paradise for birdwatchers.

Pakistan is home to the Indus River, one of the world's longest rivers, which offers chances for river rafting and boating excursions. With its exhilarating rapids and magnificent landscape, the Gilgit-Baltistan segment of the river close to Skardu is a particularly well-liked spot for rafting.

Coastal Regions and Beaches

The Arabian Sea coastline of Pakistan has scenic beaches, peaceful coastal communities, and chances for leisure and water sports. The nation's coastline is renowned for its warm seas, fine sand beaches, and mouthwatering seafood.

In Karachi, Clifton Beach is a well-liked beach location for both residents and visitors. With its amusement parks, food stands, and horseback and camel rides along the sandy beaches, it creates a lively environment. The beach is the perfect location to take in the sunset and delectable regional cuisine.

In Balochistan, there lies a hidden treasure called Ormara Beach, which is renowned for its pristine beauty and serenity. The beach provides a tranquil getaway from the hectic city life and is flanked by impressive rocks.

Small, deserted Astola Island, often called "Island of the Seven Hills," is located off the coast of Balochistan. With its beautiful coral reefs and varied marine life, it is a protected area and a snorkelers and divers' paradise.

Dunes and Deserts

Huge deserts and captivating dunes may be found in Pakistan, which creates an extraordinary and fantastical scene. These dry areas provide opportunities for camel rides, desert safaris, and stargazing beneath the open sky at night.

The biggest desert in Pakistan is the Thar Desert, which is situated in the southeast of the nation. It crosses both Pakistan and India and is renowned for its gleaming dunes, traditional desert settlements, and vibrant Thari cultural heritage.

Punjab province is home to the Cholistan Desert, often called the "Derawar Desert." It is distinguished for its vast dunes, historic forts, and the nomadic way of life of the indigenous populations. Every year, the spectacular off-road racing Cholistan Desert Rally draws spectators from all over the globe.

Caves and Waterfalls

Inspiring waterfalls and mysterious tunnels that display the force of nature and provide chances for exploration and adventure may be found across Pakistan.

Beautiful waterfalls like the Kutton Waterfall and the enchanting Ratti Gali

Lake can be found in Azad Jammu and Kashmir's Neelum Valley. These flowing waterfalls, which are encircled by verdant woods, are ideal for nature lovers and photographers.

A refreshing getaway from the city is provided by the Pir Sohawa Waterfall, a hidden jewel in the Margalla Hills close to Islamabad. A little trek will bring you to the waterfall, which offers a peaceful setting for picnics and leisure.

Several spectacular caverns, like the Takht Bhai caverns in Khyber Pakhtunkhwa and the Kot Diji Caves in Sindh, may be found in Pakistan. Archaeologically significant, these caverns provide a window into the country's early history and cultures.

In conclusion, Pakistan's natural beauty and outdoor experiences provide a paradise for outdoor lovers and thrill-seekers. The nation provides a wide variety of adventures for everyone to enjoy, from hiking and trekking in the gorgeous mountains to visiting national parks, taking part in water sports, and finding secret caverns. Pakistan's natural wonders will astound tourists with their unparalleled beauty and grandeur, whether it be the exhilaration of climbing, the tranquility of lakes and rivers, the splendor of beaches and deserts, or the awe-inspiring sight of waterfalls and caverns.

Chapter 7: Traditional Foods and Regional Specialties

Pakistan is well known for its extensive and varied culinary traditions, which provide a mouthwatering variety of tastes, spices, and fragrant foods. Pakistani cuisine is a mash-up of tastes, fusing the finest of South Asian, Central Asian, and Middle Eastern culinary traditions. It is influenced by its rich history and unique cultural background. Pakistani cuisine is a great joy for food lovers, with everything from scrumptious sweets and cool drinks to juicy kebabs and curries. Let's look at the traditional foods, street foods, drinks, and dining traditions that make Pakistani food so distinctive.

Well-known Pakistani Recipes

The rich and intense tastes of Pakistani food are well-known, and slow cooking methods, spices, and herbs are also heavily used. The following cuisines from Pakistan are well-known and must be tried:

- Biryani: Made with basmati rice, meat (often chicken, beef, or mutton), and a combination of fragrant spices, biryani is a flavorful rice dish. Layers of cooking provide a rich, fragrant meal that is often topped with fried onions, mint, and coriander.

- Nihari: Nihari is a Mughal-era dish that is a slow-cooked pork stew. Usually prepared with beef or lamb, bone marrow is cooked with it, and a mixture of spices is used to flavor it. Nihari is often eaten with naan (traditional bread) and topped with fresh lemon juice, fried onions, and ginger.

- A popular meal known as karahi is prepared with a tool similar to a wok. It is prepared using tomatoes, onions, ginger, garlic, and a mixture of spices and may be made with beef, mutton, or chicken. Rich, spicy tastes make karahi popular.

- Samosa: In Pakistan, samosas are a well-known snack food item. It is a pastry that has been deep-fried and then filled with a flavorful stew of spiced potatoes, peas, and sometimes minced meat. Samosas are a traditional teatime snack that is often served with chutneys (sauces).

- Chapli Kebab: This savory and juicy kebab, which hails from the Khyber Pakhtunkhwa area, is cooked with minced meat (often beef or lamb) blended with several spices, onions, tomatoes, and herbs. It is often served with raita and naan.

- Haleem: Made with lentils, meat (typically beef or chicken), and wheat, haleem is a filling and nutrient-dense meal. After being slow-cooked for many hours, it has the consistency of thick, creamy porridge. Fried onions, ginger, and lemon juice are common additions to haleem garnishes.

Snacks and Street Food

The dynamic and varied street food culture of Pakistan offers a broad selection of delectable snacks and fast eats that are an authentic representation of the nation's culinary history. Here are some tasty snacks and common street cuisine to enjoy:

- Gol Gappay, sometimes referred to as Pani puri, is a popular street food snack. It comprises hollow, crispy puris that have been filled with a blend of chutneys, potatoes, chickpeas, and tart tamarind water. Every mouthful is a delicious explosion of flavors.

- Aloo Tikki is a well-known potato-based snack that is produced by shallow frying mashed potatoes along with spices and herbs. It is topped with yogurt, tamarind sauce, and chaat masala and is accompanied by a variety of chutneys.

- Samosa Chaat: Made with crumbled samosas, chickpeas, yogurt, chutneys, and spices, Samosa Chaat is a delectable snack. It is a savory snack that gives the ideal harmony of acidic, sweet, and spicy tastes.

- Bun Kabab: A desi burger is called a bun kabab. It comprises a tasty, spicy meat patty (often beef or chicken) served on a soft bun with a variety of sauces, onions, and chutneys.

- Fruit Chaat: Made with a variety of seasonal fruits, including apples, oranges, pomegranates, and bananas, Fruit Chaat is a light and healthful street food snack. Chaat masala, a sour spice blend, lemon juice, and sometimes yogurt are added to the fruits before serving.

Customary Drinks and Foods

There are several traditional drinks and beverages available in Pakistan that are great for soothing thirst and offering a cool break from the heat. Here are a few well-liked classic beverages:

- Lassi: A traditional yogurt-based beverage, lassi is available in a variety of tastes, such as plain, sweet, and salty. It is produced by combining yogurt, water, and sometimes salt or sugar. A popular beverage to combat the summer heat is lassi, which is often consumed with meals.

- Sugarcane Juice: Made from freshly squeezed sugarcane, sugarcane juice is a delicious and energizing beverage. It is a common option during the hot summer months and is often served with a squeeze of lemon.

- Kahwa: Cardamom, cinnamon, saffron, and almonds are some of the flavorful ingredients that are added to this traditional Kashmiri green tea. It is often served in little cups with a dash of honey and is renowned for its calming and warming qualities.

- Sherbet is a sweet, fruity beverage that is produced by combining water with fruit syrups or concentrates. There are several tastes available, including rose, lemon, and orange. Sherbet is a popular beverage during festive events and is often served cold.

Food Manners and Dining Rituals

To respect and appreciate the cuisine and culture while eating in Pakistan, it is important to follow specific etiquette and traditions. To remember while eating, consider the following:

1. Eating with your hands is customary in many areas of Pakistan, especially while devouring regional specialties like biryani, naan, and kebabs. But cutlery is also often used, particularly in more formal situations.

2. Shoes & Footwear: It's polite to take your shoes off before entering a traditional restaurant or someone's house. This procedure guarantees cleanliness and demonstrates courtesy for the host.

3. Sharing Food: Hospitality and sharing food are important aspects of Pakistani culture. It is typical to eat together as a group with the plates being placed in the middle and everyone helping themselves. Food sharing helps to promote community and connection.

4. Respecting seniors: In Pakistani culture, it is traditional to give seniors priority while receiving meals. It is customary to hold off on starting to eat until the oldest member at the table has done so.

Pakistani food is a celebration of the tastes, spices, and cooking customs that have developed through the years. Pakistani cuisine is a fascinating voyage for the taste buds, from the rich and fragrant biryanis to the delicious street food, cool drinks, and the warmth of traditional dining rituals. To appreciate Pakistan's cultural and gastronomic history, one must sample the wide variety of cuisines, street snacks, and drinks available there. So, savor the tastes of Pakistan and allow the food to take you on an unforgettable gastronomic journey.

Chapter 8: Purchases and Souvenirs

Pakistan offers a vast variety of traditional handicrafts, artwork, and one-of-a-kind souvenirs, making it a treasure trove for shoppers and art lovers. Pakistan offers a dynamic shopping experience that highlights the nation's rich cultural history and craftsmanship, from busy marketplaces and bazaars to contemporary retail complexes and centers. Let's examine Pakistan's retail scene, including its traditional handicrafts, well-known marketplaces, shopping centers, and the distinctive trinkets you may bring home.

Traditional Crafts and Visual Arts

Pakistan is well known for its excellent traditional artwork and handicrafts, which represent the nation's rich cultural past. These handicrafts are evidence of the exceptional creativity and workmanship of the regional craftspeople. Here are some examples of traditional Pakistani artwork and handicrafts:

1. Woodwork: Pakistan is known for its intricately carved wooden sculptures, furniture, and accessories. The woodwork from Punjab's Chiniot district is renowned for its unique patterns and expert workmanship.

2. Ceramics & Pottery: The Punjabi city of Multan is well-known for its blue ceramics. Intricate blue patterns are used to create exquisite ceramics in this ancient art style. Vases, plates, and tiles made of ceramic are popular purchases.

3. Pakistan is well-known for its colorful and exquisite embroidered work. You may get a broad variety of embroidered fabrics,

including shawls, scarves, bedspreads, and clothing, from the vibrant and intricate Phulkari embroidery of Punjab to the mirror work and Sindhi embroidery of Sindh province.

4. Rugs & Carpets: Pakistani carpets and rugs are widely coveted due to their superior quality and workmanship. The elaborate patterns and vibrant colors of the handmade carpets from towns like Lahore and Peshawar, which often include traditional themes, are well recognized.

5. Metalwork: The brass and copper artwork produced in Wazirabad is famous. Beautiful trays, bowls, vases, and ornamental objects made of brass and copper are made by talented artists.

Bazaars and Markets

The shopping trip must include visiting Pakistan's lively marketplaces and bazaars. These vibrant markets are hives of activity and sell a variety of goods, including traditional handicrafts, apparel, spices, and jewelry. The following Pakistani bazaars and marketplaces are well-known:

- One of Lahore's oldest and most well-known marketplaces is called Anarkali Bazaar. A large variety of goods are available there, including apparel, jewelry, handicrafts, and traditional shoes (chassis). It is a bustling shopping area. The market is renowned for its vibrant decorations and jovial atmosphere.

- Empress Market in Karachi is a historic market that goes back to the British period. It is situated in the city's center. You may buy a wide range of goods there, including fresh vegetables, spices, clothes, accessories, and handicrafts.

- Saddar Bazaar, in Peshawar: The crowded Saddar Bazaar in Peshawar is well-known for its antiques, carpets, handicrafts, and traditional Afghan jewelry. For those looking for distinctive and genuine Pashtun artwork and antiquities, it is a treasure trove.

Shopping Centers and Malls

Pakistan is home to contemporary shopping malls and centers that meet the demands and desires of consumers in addition to traditional marketplaces and bazaars. These malls provide a variety of domestic and foreign brands, as well as entertainment venues and food courts, making for a pleasant and easy shopping experience. Here are a few of Pakistan's well-known retail centers:

- One of Pakistan's biggest and most opulent malls, Centaurus Mall is situated in the nation's capital, Islamabad. Along with a theater, food court, and entertainment options, it is home to several regional and worldwide companies.

- Dolmen Mall in Karachi is a well-liked retail area that has a variety of clothing brands, accessories, gadgets, and culinary establishments. It is renowned for its chic and contemporary atmosphere.

- Packages Mall, Lahore: Packages Mall is a cutting-edge retail center that meets a variety of customer demands. It has a variety of domestic and foreign brands, a multiplex theater, and a special food court.

Special Merchandise to Take Home

There are a variety of unusual mementos that you may purchase in Pakistan to preserve the memory of your journey. These trinkets not only serve as keepsakes but also help to highlight the rich cultural history of the nation. Here are some unusual keepsakes to think about:

1. Pashmina Shawls: Known for their warmth and tenderness, Pashmina shawls are made of the finest wool. They are finely woven and often have lovely needlework. Pashmina shawls are opulent gifts that people treasure.

2. Ajrak: The traditional block-printed fabric known as ajrak represents Sindhi culture. It is often colored with natural colors and has elaborate geometric designs. Tablecloths, scarves, and stoles made of ajrak are preferred gifts.

3. Miniature paintings are a distinctive art style that dates back to the Mughal dynasty. The scenarios from epics, myths, and royal courts are depicted in these minutely detailed paintings. They make stunning home décor items and mementos.

4. Sindhri Mangoes: Popularly referred to as the "King of Mangoes," Sindhri mangoes are grown in Pakistan and are prized for their succulent sweetness. These mangoes are in great demand and make a delectable food gift.

6. Handmade Jewelry: The beautiful jewelry designs from Pakistan are well-known. You may discover a broad selection of handcrafted jewelry that embodies the cultural history of the nation, ranging from classic silver and gold jewelry to pieces adorned with semi-precious stones.

Finally, shopping in Pakistan is a lovely way to experience the workmanship and rich cultural legacy of the nation. Pakistan offers something for every consumer, from exclusive souvenirs to colorful marketplaces, contemporary shopping centers, and traditional handicrafts and artwork. Explore the vivid colors and skilled workmanship of the busy marketplaces while taking something of Pakistan's cultural heritage home with you to treasure forever.

Chapter 9: Transportation Within Pakistan

To meet your requirements and tastes, a variety of transportation options are available inside Pakistan. There are many ways to get about Pakistan, whether you like the ease of flying, the picturesque lines provided by railroads, the affordability of buses, or the adaptability of taxis and ride-sharing services. Let's examine the various transportation options in Pakistan.

Internal Air Travel

Long-distance domestic flights are a common means of transportation in Pakistan. The nation has an extensive network of airports that connects both populated areas and outlying regions. When traveling between faraway areas, domestic flights are convenient since they save you time and effort. Pakistan International Airlines (PIA), Airblue, and SereneAir are a few of the main carriers that fly inside Pakistan. These airlines provide routine flights with cozy seats and a variety of amenities to make flying easy. When traveling between cities like Karachi, Lahore, Islamabad, Peshawar, and Quetta, domestic flights are very practical.

Railroads and Trains

Within Pakistan, you may travel in style and at a reasonable price thanks to the train network. A substantial rail system run by Pakistan Railways connects the nation's main cities and communities. You can see the beautiful scenery and learn about the local culture while traveling by train. The train network provides a range of lodging options, such as air-conditioned sleeping cabins, air-conditioned and non-air-conditioned seats, and economy-class seating. The Karachi-Lahore, Lahore-Islamabad, and Peshawar-Quetta railway lines are a few of Pakistan's most well-traveled ones. It's a good idea to purchase rail tickets in advance, particularly during periods of high travel demand.

Coaches and Buses

Within Pakistan, buses and coaches are popular and affordable forms of transportation for both short and long trips. Bus travel is a practical choice because of the nation's well-developed network of motorways and road infrastructure. All around the nation, several private bus operators provide cozy, air-conditioned buses with various degrees of facilities. Some of the well-known bus companies in Pakistan are Daewoo Express, Faisal Movers, and Niazi Express. These buses provide transportation between important cities, villages, and well-known tourist attractions. For shorter routes inside cities and towns, local buses and minibusses are furthermore available.

Ride-Sharing and Taxi Services

Traveling throughout Pakistan's cities and towns is flexible and convenient thanks to taxis and ride-sharing services. Taxis are easily accessible and may be booked through phone applications or by hailing one on the street. In places like Karachi and Lahore, classic yellow cabs are a regular sight. The popularity of ride-sharing services like Uber and Careem, which provide dependable and convenient transportation choices, has increased recently. Through smartphone apps, you may simply arrange a ride and follow its progress using these services. In Pakistan's largest cities, ride-sharing services are accessible, offering a convenient and secure form of transportation.

It is crucial to remember that to prevent any disagreements, it is best to negotiate the fee or make sure the meter is utilized while utilizing taxis or ride-sharing services. To protect your safety and security, it is also advised to choose reliable taxi services and authorized ride-sharing services.

There are several choices for transportation inside Pakistan to accommodate various travel requirements and tastes. Pakistan's transportation system makes it possible to easily see the nation whether you decide to fly, travel by picturesque rail, board a comfy bus, or select the adaptability of taxis and ride-sharing services. When deciding on the best means of transportation for your trip, take into account the distance, price, convenience, and experience you want to have. Navigating Pakistan's varied landscapes and dynamic towns becomes a pleasurable part of your trip experience because of the country's well-connected network of domestic airlines, trains, buses, and taxis.

Chapter 10: Pakistan's Accommodation Options

There is a vast variety of lodging available in Pakistan to suit various travel needs, interests, and price ranges. Pakistan provides a wide range of accommodations to fit any traveler's interests, whether they are searching for five-star hotels and resorts, affordable guesthouses and hostels, immersive homestays, and farm stays, or the daring experience of camping and glamping. Let's examine the many lodging choices Pakistan has to offer.

Resorts and Inns

There are several hotels and resorts in Pakistan that provide guests with comfort, luxury and a wide range of services. Hotels owned and run locally as well as by well-known worldwide hotel chains can be found in major towns including Peshawar, Karachi, Lahore, and Islamabad. These institutions provide a broad choice of amenities and services, including as tastefully furnished rooms, dining options, spas, fitness centers, swimming pools, and meeting spaces.

Luxury resorts may also be located in picturesque areas all across the nation, providing a retreat-like experience surrounded by the grandeur of the natural world. Numerous of these resorts have individual villas, breathtaking vistas, and access to outdoor pursuits like hiking, birding, and animal viewing. Serena Hotels, Marriott Hotels, and Pearl Continental Hotels are a few of the well-known hotel and resort brands in Pakistan.

Hostels and Guesthouses

Guesthouses and hostels are popular options for tourists on a budget or looking for a more personal and cozy setting. These lodging options include cozy rooms, common areas, and a chance to mingle with other tourists.

Both urban and rural parts of Pakistan have guesthouses, which provide a warm and individualized experience. They are often managed by local families that provide friendly hospitality and local knowledge. Guesthouses are a fantastic way to get to know the community and enjoy true Pakistani hospitality. Additionally, some guesthouses provide home-cooked meals, enhancing the genuine experience.

Hostels are the perfect choice for lone travelers or those looking for a lively, sociable environment, especially in big cities and well-known tourist areas. These facilities provide dormitory-style lodging, sometimes with shared amenities including kitchens, common spaces, and scheduled activities. Hostels are a fantastic place to meet other travelers, swap stories, and get travel advice.

Homestays and Farm Stays

Homestays and farm stays provide a special chance to stay with local families and learn about their way of life for an immersed cultural experience. Homestays provide you the opportunity to stay with a local family, share meals, take part in everyday activities, and learn about their traditions and customs. This kind of lodging promotes cross-cultural interaction and offers a better knowledge of the neighborhood.

Through farm stays, you may spend time on agricultural properties where you can engage in farming activities, learn about farming procedures, and take in the peace of rural areas. Comfortable lodging is available at many farm stays, often in the form of old-fashioned cottages or guesthouses. They provide a tranquil haven away from the busy metropolis, letting you get in touch with nature and appreciate life at a slower pace.

Camping and Glamping

Camping and glamping opportunities are available in many picturesque spots around Pakistan for nature lovers and adventurers. Camping enables you to fully appreciate Pakistan's many landscapes, including its mountains, valleys, deserts, and coastal regions. You may set up your tent in specified camping areas and national parks and engage in outdoor pursuits like hiking, stargazing, and animal watching. Local retailers or outdoor adventure firms rent or sell camping supplies.

A more opulent and pleasant camping experience is offered by glamping, a blend of elegance with outdoor activities. Glamping locations include luxuries like cozy mattresses, private baths, and kitchens.

Traditional tents are one kind of glamping lodging, while safari-style lodges or eco-friendly cottages are additional options. You may appreciate nature's beauty while glamping without sacrificing comfort.

It is important to remember that it is crucial to respect the environment, adhere to local laws, and leave no trace while camping or glamping in natural regions. When visiting distant or less-traveled locations, always take precautions for your safety and ask local authorities or knowledgeable guides for guidance.

Pakistan has a wide variety of lodging choices to fit any traveler's needs and budget. Everyone can find somewhere to stay, whether they like five-star hotels and resorts, affordable guesthouses and hostels, immersive homestays and farm stays, or daring camping and glamping excursions. Choose a sort of lodging that fits your travel preferences, desired degree of comfort, and the kind of experience you're looking for. Pakistan makes sure that your visit is pleasant and memorable with its kind hospitality and beautiful scenery.

Chapter 11: Advise and Cultural Etiquette

To guarantee a respectful and pleasurable trip, it is crucial to get knowledgeable about local culture and traditions before visiting Pakistan. Following some etiquette rules will help you interact with people, manage social situations, and show respect for the traditions and customs of Pakistan, a varied nation with a rich cultural background. Here are some cultural considerations and packing advice for your trip to Pakistan.

Salutations and Social Manners

In social contacts in Pakistan, greetings are significant. It is polite to extend a cordial handshake when meeting someone for the first time while keeping eye contact. Men may also extend a respectful handshake by putting their right hand over their hearts. It is advisable to wait for someone of the opposing gender to start the greeting when addressing them. Additionally, it is considered polite to address someone with honorific titles such as "Mr." or "Mrs." before their last name.

Pakistani culture places great importance on hospitality, therefore it's typical for folks to give visitors tea or other refreshments. Such invitations should be accepted politely, and you should always thank them for their hospitality. Be careful to follow the tradition of taking off your shoes before entering someone's house.

Modesty and Dress Code

Pakistan is an Islamic nation, hence modest attire is highly valued there. It is advised to wear modest clothing, particularly while visiting places of worship or politically conservative locations. Women should stay away from wearing clothing that is too tight or exposing and instead choose loose-fitting clothes that cover their shoulders, arms, and legs. It is also advised to cover your head with a scarf or shawl while going inside mosques or other places of worship. Men have to dress modestly as well, refraining from wearing shorts and sleeveless shirts in public.

To prevent offense or discomfort, it is crucial to obey local dress codes and traditions. Dressing modestly demonstrates respect for the host culture and aids in a successful cultural exchange.

Communication and Language

Pakistan's official language is Urdu, although English is also extensively spoken and understood, particularly in metropolitan areas. It is beneficial to acquire a few fundamental Urdu words to make conversation easier and demonstrate your interest in the local tongue. The locals will often thank you for making the effort to learn their language.

Maintaining a courteous tone is crucial while speaking with Pakistanis. Avoid sensitive or divisive subjects like religion and politics until the conversation organically leads to them. When addressing someone, use suitable titles. Talking to people and showing genuine interest in their culture and customs can help you make friends with Pakistanis, who are typically cordial and pleasant.

Religious Customs and Protocol

In Pakistan, where Islam is the most common religion, religious customs, and traditions are highly valued. It is important to follow particular etiquette while visiting mosques or other religious buildings. Be mindful of ongoing prayers or religious rites by dressing modestly, taking off your shoes before entering the mosque, and dressing modestly. In mosques, it is traditional to ask permission before taking pictures, and in certain circumstances, photography may even be outright forbidden.

It's crucial to show respect to individuals who are fasting during the holy month of Ramadan when Muslims fast from dawn until sunset. Avoid eating, drinking, or smoking in public while it's still light out, and ask someone for recommendations on where to dine at this time. It is also wise to avoid planning significant gatherings or activities that could interfere with the locals' religious practices.

Safety Precautions and Ethical Tourism

When visiting Pakistan, it's crucial to put your safety first, just as when visiting any other place. To guarantee a secure and pleasurable trip, familiarize yourself with the regional laws, traditions, and cultural norms. Consider the following safety recommendations:

1. Keep up with the latest political and security developments in the places you want to visit. Consult with local authorities or your embassy if necessary, and look up travel warnings.

2. To prevent any pointless disputes or misunderstandings, respect local traditions and customs.

3. Be careful with your valuables and personal property. Keep things safe, and refrain from flaunting riches or expensive objects in public.

4. Make use of trustworthy, certified transportation providers. If using a cab, go with a reputed company or make

transportation arrangements with your lodging.

5. Keep yourself hydrated, especially in hot and arid areas, and take any essential measures for your health, such as wearing sunscreen, carrying bug repellent, and taking any prescribed medicines.

6. Respect the environment, animals, and local communities when you travel responsibly. Avoid trash, patronize regional shops and craftspeople, and practice sustainable travel.

7. You may guarantee a satisfying and unforgettable experience when visiting Pakistan by following these safety precautions and exhibiting respect for the native way of life.

When visiting Pakistan, it is essential to comprehend and adhere to local etiquette and travel recommendations. You can engage in meaningful cultural exchanges, forge relationships with the locals, and experience the hospitality and warmth of Pakistan's rich cultural heritage by bowing respectfully to people, dressing modestly, communicating clearly, respecting religious practices, and putting your safety first. Accepting the nation's cultural variety and customs improves your travels and promotes a greater appreciation for Pakistan's natural beauty and its people.

Chapter 12: Events and Festivals

Pakistan is renowned for having several exciting festivals and events. The nation provides a calendar full of vibrant and happy occasions, from religious feasts to national holidays, local festivals, and spectacular sporting events. You may experience the Pakistani people as a whole, see traditions and rituals from the past, and immerse yourself in the local culture by attending these festivals and events. Here are a few of the notable Pakistani holidays and celebrations.

Muslim Holidays

Pakistan, an Islamic nation, observes several important Islamic holidays that are very significant from both a religious and cultural standpoint. These Islamic holidays, which are celebrated with tremendous passion and excitement, are based on the lunar calendar.

The holy month of Ramadan, the name "Sweet Eid," concludes Eid al-Fitr. Families join together during this happy and festive season to exchange presents and indulge in mouthwatering traditional treats. Special prayers are offered at mosques to start the day, which is thereafter filled with celebratory dinners and get-togethers.

The "Festival of Sacrifice," also known as Eid al-Adha, honors Prophet Ibrahim's readiness to offer his son as a sacrifice to God. It entails the slaughter of animals, usually sheep or goats, and the distribution of the meat to close relatives, friends, and those in need. The holiday offers a chance for group prayers, eating, and charitable deeds.

The day known as Milad un-Nabi, sometimes referred to as Eid-e-Milad commemorates the birth of the Prophet Muhammad. Processions, religious gatherings, and the recital of poetry and songs honoring the Prophet's life and teachings commemorate the event.

Public Holidays and Other National Events

Numerous national holidays and festivals are observed in Pakistan to honor important moments in its history and culture. The Pakistani people may unite, contemplate, and show their patriotism over these holidays.

On March 23, Pakistan Day is observed to honor the Lahore Resolution, which was passed in 1940 and cleared the way for the establishment of an independent Muslim state. Parades, flag-raising ceremonies, cultural performances, and speeches celebrating the nation's accomplishments and goals commemorate the day.

The day Pakistan became independent from British domination in 1947 is commemorated as Independence Day, which falls on August 14. With flag-raising ceremonies, fireworks, cultural performances, and demonstrations of patriotic pride, the day is observed with considerable fervor.

On September 6th, Defense Day honors the tenacity and valor of the Pakistani military forces during the 1965 Indo-Pak War. Special prayers, military parades, and ceremonies are held on this day to commemorate the armed troops' sacrifices.

Local and Regional Celebrations

Pakistan has a wide variety of regional and local festivals that highlight the cultural diversity of the many regions and communities within the nation, in addition to national and religious holidays. Traditional music, dancing, handicrafts, gastronomy, and live demonstrations of local customs and traditions are features of these festivals.

The Basant holiday, which is largely observed in the Punjabi region, ushers in spring. Known as the "Festival of Kites," it is a period when kite flying events are held and the sky is covered with a rainbow of colored kites. The celebration features traditional Punjabi food feasts, dancing displays, and music.

The annual Shandur Polo Festival, which takes place in the Shandur Pass in Gilgit-Baltistan, is a spectacular sports occasion that highlights the game of polo. The event, sometimes referred to as the "Roof of the World," draws polo fans from all across the nation and provides an exceptional chance to see exciting matches against the mesmerizing Himalayan mountain range.

The Kalash people of Khyber Pakhtunkhwa celebrate the Kalash Spring Festival, a vivid and colorful occasion that heralds the start of spring. The Kalash community's distinctive culture and religious practices are on display during the festival, which include traditional music, dancing, and religious ceremonies.

Sports Competitions and Events

Pakistani culture places a high value on sports, and the nation has a long history of hosting and taking part in numerous sporting events and tournaments. Pakistan has produced world-class athletes and teams in several of the most prominent sports, including hockey, squash, polo, cricket, and squash.

Unquestionably, cricket is the most popular sport in Pakistan, and matches involving the home side are very popular and well-attended. A significant athletic occasion, the Pakistan Super Competition (PSL) is a professional Twenty20 cricket competition that brings together national and international talent for a thrilling campaign.

Another popular sport in Pakistan is hockey, which has a long history of success there. Field hockey competitions between Pakistan and India, the country's arch-rival, are eagerly anticipated occasions. Pakistan has won several Olympic medals and World Cups in the sport.

Pakistan has a significant following for the British India-born sport of squash. World-famous squash players that have dominated the sport's international circuit for decades have come from this nation. Top-ranked players from all around the globe attend the annual Pakistan Open Squash Championship.

Polo is a key part of Pakistani sports culture in addition to these other sports. The nation hosts several polo competitions, including the famed Pakistan Polo Cup, which highlights the prowess and fervor of both domestic and foreign polo players.

Pakistan's festivals and events provide a window into the nation's rich cultural past, religious traditions, sense of pride in the nation, and sports ability. These occasions provide a chance to see the variety and friendliness of the Pakistani people, whether it is via the joyful festivities of Islamic festivals, the patriotic fervor of national holidays, the cultural dynamism of regional festivals, or the excitement of sporting events. Travelers may establish relationships with the local people, make enduring memories by taking part in these festivals and events, and have a greater understanding of Pakistan's rich cultural heritage.

Chapter 13: Useful Phrases and Basic Urdu Vocabulary

When traveling to Pakistan, learning a few basic phrases and words in Urdu, the national language, can greatly enhance your interactions with the locals and make your experience more enjoyable. While many Pakistanis also speak English, making an effort to communicate in Urdu shows respect for the culture and can help you navigate daily situations more easily. Here are some useful phrases and basic Urdu vocabulary that can be handy during your visit to Pakistan.

Greetings and Polite Expressions:
Assalamu Alaikum: Peace be upon you (Islamic greeting)
Adaab: Greetings (more formal)

Shukriya: Thank you
Khuda Hafiz: Goodbye (literally, "May God be your guardian")
Bara Meherbani: Please
Aap se mil kar khushi hui: Nice to meet you

Basic Conversational Phrases:

Kya aap English bolte hain?: Do you speak English?
Mujhe Urdu nahi aati: I don't speak Urdu.
Main samajhta/samajhti hoon: I understand (male/female)
Main nahi samajhta/samajhti hoon: I don't understand (male/female)
Kya yahan kisi ko English aati hai?: Does anyone here speak English?

Directions and Getting Around:
Kidhar jaana hai? Where do you want to go?
Kitna door hai? How far is it?
Seedha jaye: Go straight
Baaye: Left

Daaye: Right
Yahaan rokiye: Stop here

Ordering Food and Drinks:
Kya khana pasand karoge?: What would you like to eat?
Ek chai, shukriya: One tea, please
Menu dikhaiye: Show me the menu
Bill, shukriya: The bill, please
Meetha: Sweet
Namkeen: Savory

Numbers:
Ek: One
Do: Two
Teen: Three
Chaar: Four
Paanch: Five
Chhah: Six
Saat: Seven
Aath: Eight
Nau: Nine
Das: Ten

Basic Nouns:
Kitab: Book
Roti: Bread
Paani: Water
Gadi: Car
Hospital: Hospital
Dukaan: Shop
Masjid: Mosque
Baazaar: Market
Station: Station
Hotel: Hotel

Basic Adjectives:
Achha: Good
Bura: Bad
Sundar: Beautiful
Meetha: Sweet
Thanda: Cold
Garam: Hot
Bada: Big
Chhota: Small
Naya: New
Purana: Old

Basic Verbs:
Karna: To do
Jana: To go
Khana: To eat
Peena: To drink
Dekhna: To see
Bolna: To speak
Sunna: To listen
Samajhna: To understand
Padhna: To read
Likha: To write

Remember, pronunciation is key when using these phrases and vocabulary. It is advisable to listen to native speakers or use language learning resources to practice the correct pronunciation. The locals will appreciate your efforts to communicate in Urdu and will be more willing to assist you.

While these phrases and vocabulary are basic, they can serve as a foundation for further language learning during your stay in Pakistan. Being able to communicate even a little in Urdu will not only make your trip more enjoyable but also foster cultural connections and create memorable experiences with the warm and hospitable people of Pakistan.

Chapter 14: Emergency Information

When traveling to any destination, it is important to be prepared for unexpected situations and have access to emergency services. Pakistan is no exception, and being aware of emergency numbers, medical facilities, and consulate services can provide peace of mind and ensure your safety during your visit. Here is some vital information regarding emergencies in Pakistan.

Emergency Numbers and Contacts

In case of an emergency, knowing the appropriate contact numbers is crucial. Here are some important emergency numbers in Pakistan:

Police Emergency: 15

Ambulance Service: 115
Fire Brigade: 16
Traffic Police: 1915
Highway Emergency Helpline: 130
Tourist Police Helpline: +92-51-9207895

It is advisable to program these numbers into your mobile phone for quick access. In an emergency, staying calm and providing clear information to the authorities can help expedite the response.

Medical Facilities and Services

Access to medical facilities and services is essential when facing health emergencies. Pakistan has a network of hospitals, clinics, and medical professionals across the country. Here are some key points to keep in mind:

1. Hospitals: Major cities in Pakistan have well-equipped hospitals with emergency

departments. Some renowned hospitals include Aga Khan University Hospital in Karachi, Shaukat Khanum Memorial Cancer Hospital & Research Centre in Lahore, and Pakistan Institute of Medical Sciences (PIMS) in Islamabad.

2. Medical Services: In addition to hospitals, there are private clinics and medical centers that provide a range of services, including general check-ups, specialized treatments, and emergency care. It is advisable to have travel insurance that covers medical expenses and to carry a copy of your insurance documents.

3. Pharmacies: Pharmacies, known as "medical stores" or "chemist shops" in Pakistan, can be found throughout cities and towns. It is advisable to carry a basic first aid kit and any necessary medications with you during your travels.

4. Vaccinations: Before traveling to Pakistan, it is recommended to consult your healthcare provider or a travel clinic to receive necessary vaccinations and medications. Common vaccines for travelers to Pakistan may include those for hepatitis A and B, typhoid, polio, and tetanus.

5. Travel Insurance: It is highly recommended to have travel insurance that covers medical emergencies, evacuation, and repatriation. Familiarize yourself with the terms and conditions of your insurance policy, including contact details for emergency assistance.

In case of a medical emergency, dial the local emergency number and provide clear information about the situation and your location. The emergency services will guide you and dispatch appropriate medical help.

Consulates and Embassies

Consulates and embassies play a crucial role in providing assistance to foreign nationals in times of need. If you encounter any legal issues, lose your passport, or require consular services, it is important to be aware of the location and contact information of your country's embassy or consulate in Pakistan. Here are some key points to remember:

1. Embassies and High Commissions: Major countries have embassies or high commissions in Islamabad, the capital city of Pakistan. These diplomatic missions provide consular services and support to their citizens. Additionally, some countries may have consulates in other major cities such as Karachi and Lahore.

2. Contact Information: Before your trip, make a note of the contact details of your embassy or consulate in Pakistan. This includes the address, phone number, and

emergency contact information. Registering with your embassy or consulate upon arrival is also recommended.

3. Consular Services: Consulates and embassies can assist with a range of services, including passport replacement, legal assistance, and emergency evacuation. It is advisable to carry a copy of your passport and other important travel documents in case of loss or theft.

4. Safety and Security: Embassies and consulates often provide travel advisories and safety information for their citizens. It is important to stay updated on any security alerts or advisories issued by your embassy or consulate during your stay in Pakistan.

4. Local Representation: In addition to foreign embassies, many countries have honorary consulates in various cities in Pakistan. These honorary consulates may

offer limited consular services and can be a source of assistance if needed.

It is recommended to familiarize yourself with the location and services provided by your embassy or consulate in Pakistan before your trip. In case of an emergency or when in need of consular assistance, contact your embassy or consulate immediately.

Being aware of emergency information is crucial when traveling to Pakistan. Memorizing or storing emergency contact numbers, knowing the location of medical facilities, and having access to consular services can provide reassurance and support during unforeseen circumstances. Remember to prioritize your safety and well-being, follow local laws and regulations, and stay informed about any travel advisories or updates provided by your embassy or consulate. With adequate preparation and knowledge, you can enjoy your time in Pakistan with peace of mind.

PAKISTAN TRAVEL GUIDE 2023

Conclusion

In conclusion, tourists seeking an educational and interesting trip can find a wide variety of activities and attractions in Pakistan. Pakistan has a lot to offer every kind of tourist, from its breathtaking natural vistas to its rich history, lively culture, and kind hospitality.

We have looked at many different areas of Pakistan in this travel guide, including its geography, climate, history, culture, politics, government, and economics. The many regions, significant cities, historical and cultural landmarks, outdoor activities, food, shopping, transit, and lodging alternatives, as well as cultural etiquette, festivals, emergency information, and helpful words, have all been covered in detail.

I sought to provide you with the information required to plan and maximize your trip to

Pakistan by offering thorough information on each subject. Pakistan has something to offer everyone, whether you are a fan of the natural world, a history buff, an adventurer, or just someone wishing to immerse themselves in a lively and hospitable society.

Despite the amazing experiences Pakistan has to offer, it is always advised to use care, be aware of your surroundings, and abide by any travel advice or recommendations given by your embassy or consulate. To promote healthy relationships and guarantee a peaceful travel experience, respect for regional norms, traditions, and cultural sensitivity is essential.

It is advised to prepare for your trip in advance, including getting the required travel papers, getting the proper travel insurance, and doing extensive research on the locations you aim to visit, as is the case with any vacation destination. Although Pakistan has been thoroughly covered in this travel guide, there is always more to learn and see. Accept the spirit of exploration and let the beauty and variety of this extraordinary nation enthrall you.

Every moment in Pakistan is a chance for exploration and connection, whether you're wandering the busy streets of Lahore, taking in the ancient remains of Taxila, setting off on an exhilarating hike through the Karakoram Mountains, or enjoying the delicacies of regional cuisine.

I hope that this travelog has motivated you to visit Pakistan on your own and has offered insightful information to improve your trip. May your trips be full of priceless experiences, cross-cultural interactions, and a profound respect for Pakistan's beauty.

Keep in mind to travel responsibly, showing respect for the local community, the environment, and cultural heritage. Take advantage of the Pakistan people's friendliness and kindness to make lifelong memories. Pakistan is eager to welcome you and share its riches with you, making your trip there absolutely unforgettable.

Have a safe trip, and have an amazing vacation in Pakistan!

Printed in Great Britain
by Amazon